HOW T

JEALOUSY

FREE

Understanding Jealousy, Its Causes, & Helping Yourself or Your Partner Defeat the Green-Eyed Monster

By Stewart Roper

Copyright:

Disclaimer Notice:

Dedication

This book is lovingly dedicated to my daughter, Siân without whose help and support this book would not have been possible.

CHAPTER 1

Introduction

Jealousy

What Is Jealousy?

The Mind

Are You Jealous?

Is Your Partner Jealous?

Fred & Jane, Susan & Dave

Introduction

In 2017, after battling with my own jealousy for many years, I decided that I would like to write a book on helping others to deal with their jealousy. I had been personally tormented with jealousy for most of my life and having read as many books on the subject as I could possibly get my hands on I discovered there wasn't a book out there to fix my problems. The few good books I came across on jealousy were rather dated and some of the newer ones were either totally inept or not even relevant as they focused too much on the need to see a psychiatrist. I couldn't find the book I was looking for. **I wanted a book that actually worked and having found none, I decided I would write the book that I wanted to read.** A book that was practical and easy to use. I wanted a book that didn't just focus on the problems that jealousy causes in a relationship, but also a book that gave answers to such questions including: What is jealousy? What causes someone to be jealous? Why is jealousy so destructive? A book that described how to spot the signs of jealousy not only in our own behaviour but in others too. It was important to me that the book not only helped people who suffer with jealousy, but also helped people who are in a relationship with a partner who suffers from jealousy. Overall, I wanted to write a book that focused upon helping people change their lives for the better.

Is this book for you? Do you suffer with jealousy? Do you constantly worry that your partner will leave you for someone else? Do you question your partner's whereabouts? Do you check your partner's private messages? Does your partner suffer with jealousy? Does your partner question your every movement? Does your partner check your private messages? If you have answered yes to any of the previous, then this is the book for you.

This book is divided in to three main sections, the first section of the book explores the origins of jealousy and why jealousy is so destructive, not only to ourselves but the people we love. The second section of the book is written for the person who suffers with jealousy themselves and is looking to change their negative ways. Finally, the third section of the book is written those of you who have a partner who suffers with jealousy. Fundamentally, this book explains how the thoughts that we see and hear in our mind, make us who we are through our actions. By being aware of how our minds work, we can channel our thoughts in a positive direction.

How To Be Jealousy Free, is to be read with an open mind and a willingness to change. The techniques within this book can be challenging and unorthodox and can only be of use if you implement the techniques into your daily life. Change your thoughts, feelings and eventually, your behaviour. Just like anything in life, you will only get out of this book what you choose to put in. If you use the techniques within this book regularly then change is inevitable. A jealous person doesn't think jealous thoughts because they are jealous. A jealous person is jealous, because they think jealous thoughts.

Stewart Roper

Jealousy

Jealousy has been part of life since life first began upon the Earth. Jealousy takes place in all forms of life not just in humans, anyone who has more than one pet can vouch for such jealous behaviour. Jealousy can infect a person at any age, a child can be jealous of a younger sibling, a parent can be jealous of their child's confidence. *"More men die of jealousy than of cancer."* Joseph. P. Kennedy. The destruction and the havoc that comes from jealousy is well documented throughout history, from philosophers, scholars, poets to every major religion. William Shakespeare wrote in *The Comedy of Errors;* "The venom clamours of a jealous woman poisons more deadly than a mad dog's tooth." If you are suffering with jealousy yourself or are in a relationship with someone who suffers with jealousy, you will know that Shakespeare wasn't far off the mark. **Jealousy seems to have a way of taking control of a person's thoughts and behaviour and turns them in to a Jekyll and Hyde type of character, where their personality becomes volatile and negative.**

"Jealousy is the jaundice of the soul." John Dryden. Without change having a happy successful relationship where jealousy is present is near impossible, a partner who doesn't trust their loved one or believe what they say, is mentally and physically draining. It becomes a relationship where the partner feels like they are constantly walking on eggshells day in, day out, it becomes in the end a relationship from hell.

Why Is Jealousy So Bad?

In the book *Jealousy* Dr Paul Hauck wrote "A loving relationship is nothing more or less than an agreement between two individuals to fulfil specific conditions for that relationship to survive."

What is it about jealousy that makes it so negative and detrimental to our lives and our loved ones? Jealousy in a relationship is like a small hole in a ship, it doesn't matter how large the ship left untreated the tiniest little hole will eventually sink the largest ship. Jealousy in a relationship will turn love to hate in no time, unless the hole is plugged, jealousy eventually eats away at everything that's good, until there is nothing left but hate. Where there is jealousy there is no trust and trust is the foundation that relationships are built upon. Trust is like the cement that holds a house together, without the cement the house will just fall apart.

Jealousy like any negative habit such as smoking, drinking or gambling is impossible to change by using willpower alone, because all our habits reside deep within the depths of our unconscious mind, beyond the reach of our conscious mind. This is why whenever someone is suffering from jealousy, it's near impossible to try and rationalise with such an individual, as the person suffering with jealousy is mainly unconscious of their jealous ways.

Most people who suffer from jealousy may seem confident and happy on the outside however, most people are battling with their private worries and concerns. One of the most destructive traits of jealousy is a controlling personality and in its worst-case scenario, jealousy can lead to abusive relationships. One has only got to pick up a newspaper or watch the evening news, to see people who have been assaulted, or even murdered by their partner because of their extreme jealous, insecure ways.

Jealousy & Health

"He that is jealous is not in love."
Saint Augustine.

Living with jealousy has a tremendous negative affect upon our physical health, ranging from the common headache, to suffering from high blood pressure that can potentially lead to heart disease. The most damaging aspect of jealousy from a physical point of view, is stress that jealousy brings within our lives. Researchers have found that stress is one of the biggest causes of cardiac arrest. Stress is also a major cause of stomach problems, such as Crohn's disease and irritable bowel syndrome.

Jealousy not only has a negative effect upon our physical health, it also has an extremely negative effect upon our mental health. If you are insecure and jealous yourself, the strain of constantly worrying if your partner's going to get back with their ex-partner or abscond with the local shop assistant, is immense. Researchers into mental health have suggested that whenever a person is suffering from one psychological problem it leads to other mental health problems, such as low self-esteem, depression, anxiety and panic attacks.

Being in a relationship with someone who is suffering with jealousy, can be just as harmful to your own mental and physical health as if you were suffering from jealousy yourself.

Jealously & Abuse

Sharing your life with someone that you love and who loves you, is one of the most joyous things in the world. Being in a relationship with someone whom you trust and who trusts you brings companionship, happiness and fulfilment. Sadly though, not all relationships are so harmonious, happy and positive. For some people their relationship with their partner has become negative, sour and toxic because of jealousy.

Extreme jealousy can lead to abuse. Whenever a person tries to control their partner by demanding what they can and can't do, who they can and can't talk to or what they can or can't wear, this is a warning sign that their attitude is in fact a form of abuse. The dividing line between jealousy and abusive behaviour is so fine that many cross the line without knowing, and once crossed, the line begins to fade fast.

Signs of abusive behaviour:

- Someone who tries to control their partner's behaviour

- Someone who makes their partner nervous

- Someone who believes that their partner belongs to them

- Someone who shouts at their partner often

- Someone who constantly puts their partner down

Slippery Slope

Abuse can be a slow and gradual development in a relationship filled with jealousy. Some people still believe that abuse is only abuse if it is physical, when in fact, the most common and overlooked form is emotional abuse. The old proverb, " Sticks and stones may break my bones but words will never hurt me," are far from the truth and according to most experts the effects of emotional abuse, and the psychological long-term ramifications for the victim of emotional abuse is far more harmful than physical abuse.

What Is Jealousy?

"You can be the moon and still be
jealous of the stars."
Gary Allan.

What is jealousy this feeling, that can make people feel and behave so strangely? This feeling that can cause so much heartache and pain. This feeling that can turn love to hate, this feeling that can turn friend to foe, this feeling that can turn good neighbours into neighbours from hell, this feeling that ends so many relationships that apart from this jealousy feeling, could have prospered. Jealousy is fundamentally FEAR that originates within the mind whenever we are insecure. **Jealousy and fear are intrinsically one and the same, they are so tightly woven together that they cannot be disconnected.** You cannot have jealousy without fear. Jealousy and fear are like happiness and love you cannot have happiness without love, they are fundamentally connected.

"Jealousy, that dragon which slays love under the pretence of keeping it alive." Havelock Ellis. A Course In Miracles, by Foundation For Inner Peace suggests the concept, that there are only two primary emotions, love and fear and all other emotions, are merely attributes to love and fear. If we are secure and happy then we must feel loved. However, if we feel insecure and jealous, we are living in fear. When we love something or someone, we feel happy, we feel positive, however when we fear something or someone, we feel unhappy, we feel negative. People who are suffering from jealousy live their lives constantly in fear. They fear that their partner will leave them one day, or they fear that their partner will run away with someone else, they fear that no matter who it is in their life, they are destined to be alone or betrayed. A person suffering with jealousy is tortured by their fears.

Jealousy is fundamentally fear that comes from within us and not from without us; fear is the reason why people suffer from jealousy. To be truly free from jealousy we must be free from fear as much as possible, for without fear jealousy cannot exist. We must replace the insecurity of fear with the security of love, to be free from jealousy.

It's All In The Mind

If jealousy is fundamentally fear, doesn't that mean that jealousy is all in the mind? That question is like asking, is love all in the mind? Whenever someone gets a feeling, be it a negative feeling such as jealousy, or a positive feeling such as love, all our feelings are the consequences of our thoughts and everything that we do in life, is first and foremost created within the mind. In fact, everything that is created by mankind is first created in the mind of the creator, from the clothes we wear to the chairs we sit on. The great inventor and entrepreneur Thomas Edison stated that he imagined all his inventions in his mind first before he created them with his hands. Our feelings and our behaviour are nothing but a reflection of our thoughts, so as to answer the question is jealousy all in the mind the answer must be YES.

As jealousy is created internally within the mind, it is therefore subjective, not objective. A person who thinks jealous thoughts behaves jealously. Our thoughts, feelings and behaviour are all connected, they are constantly influencing and affecting one another all the time. A person doesn't think jealous thoughts because they are jealous, a person is jealous because they think jealous thoughts. **Our feelings and our behaviour is a result of what we think about.** Let's go over that statement again: our feelings and our behaviour, are a result of what we think about. Jealousy comes from within not from without. That means that the neighbour's new car, or your partner's new young and attractive work colleague can't make you or anyone else jealous. WE MAKE OURSELVES JEALOUS.

Jealousy is the result of jealous thoughts, that shows itself externally through jealous behaviour and over time the person suffering from jealousy, becomes totally unaware of all the negative thoughts that lead them to feeling so insecure and jealous to begin with. Over time jealous behaviour becomes an unconscious habit just like biting our nails or smoking.

The Mind

"Jealousy ...is a mental cancer."

B. C. Forbes.

What has the mind got to do with jealousy? The mind has everything to do with jealousy or one should say jealousy has everything to do with mind. The mind is the instrument, that makes us all so unique, it is the mind that makes the difference between someone suffering with jealousy and someone not. Our mind is the dominating factor in who we are, who we have been and who we will become.

For the purpose of this book we will divide the mind into two simple concepts, the conscious mind and the unconscious mind. Many experts in the field of the mind believe that at most, we only use around 10% of our brains' potential and that small percentage that we do use resides in our conscious mind. Your conscious mind is that part of your mind that you are using right now to read this book. Our conscious mind can only focus on one thing at a time. The other 90% of our brains potential that we don't generally use, resides in our unconscious mind. Your unconscious mind is

15

the part of your mind that is busy in the background controlling all your physiological automated body functions, such as your breathing, blood pressure and your digestion functions, etc... Our unconscious mind the biggest part of our mind, strangely enough doesn't know fact from fiction; our unconscious mind is the part of the mind that never sleeps, it has no concept of time therefore it cannot tell the difference between the past, present and the future. Our unconscious mind is also where all of our fears, worries and insecurities live and hide.

A great way to envisage the mind is to use the analogy that has been around for some time now and yet it's still one of the best ways to visualise the conscious and unconscious mind. Image an iceberg floating on an ocean of water. The tip, the part of the iceberg that is visible from surface, is in fact the smallest part of the iceberg. That tip represents our conscious mind that we generally use. As with all icebergs the great majority of its mass is hidden below the water, totally invisible from above the surface. The part of the iceberg that is below the waters is like the unconscious part of our mind, that we don't generally use.

Our conscious mind cannot store information, it only filters information. It is our unconscious mind that stores information, however our unconscious mind cannot filter information.

We Mainly Think In Images

"What we think we become."
Buddha.

Our thoughts work mainly through images and associations from the memories we have stored in our unconscious mind. Try this experiment, close your eyes and try NOT to think of a RED BALLOON. Were you successful? No! Of course not. It's impossible for your conscious mind not to think of something once you become consciously aware of a particular thought. You see whenever you have a thought, your unconscious mind will turn that thought automatically into a image in your mind. So even though in the experiment you tried not to think of a red balloon, your unconscious mind automatically created an image of a red balloon for you to see.

Now close your eyes again. This time think of a GREEN BALLOON. Were you successful? Yes! Of course, you were. So, what happened in your mind when you thought of a green balloon? You more than likely saw an image in your mind's eye of a green balloon. **The interesting thing about our mind is that whatever we think about, good or bad we will see an image of that thought, in our mind.**

Over time our conscious thoughts, become unconscious thoughts, that eventually become habitual thoughts, leading to habits. When someone is jealous, they are often jealous because of the negative images they are seeing within their own mind. With this book we will learn how to create and dwell upon positive images that we choose to see, that make us feel good.

Operating On Autopilot

"Just think of happy thoughts and you will fly."
Peter Pan.

Have you ever experienced driving to a destination that you travel often to and wonder how you got there so quickly? It's as if the journey just zipped by while you cannot recollect the journey in any great detail. The reason why the journey seemed kind of hazy is because at that particular time, you weren't traveling to your destination consciously, (using your conscious mind) you were in fact, for the greater part travelling in a unconscious state (using your unconscious mind.) Your day to day conscious mind was elsewhere at that period of time, perhaps you were thinking of the party you had with your family at the weekend, or maybe you were thinking about your next fabulous holiday that you have planned. Whatever the reason, at that time whilst traveling to your destination your conscious mind wasn't really conscious (aware) of the journey.

So, how did you manage to get to your destination without crashing your vehicle? You arrived at your destination by using your autopilot, (this resides in your unconscious mind) and so allowing you to arrive safely.

Running on autopilot is something that the unconscious mind can switch to, when something that we do is done often enough it then becomes automated. Repetition builds memory. You have probably heard of the expression *"I can do it, with my eyes closed,"* most people say such a phrase in jest, when they are confident at performing a particular task or skill. When a task or skill becomes automated, it's as if the mind goes into a state of autopilot, without the need for us thinking consciously about what we are actually doing, to achieve the desired outcome; it just becomes automatic.

The same is true with a behaviour such as jealousy, whenever we repeat something often enough either positive or negative that something then becomes automatic, whether that be a skill such as driving or a negative behaviour such as jealousy. Whenever someone is insecure and jealous their thoughts, feelings and behaviour eventually run at an unconscious level; that person's behaviour then starts to function below their level of self-awareness, their jealous ways then become automated.

To be able to be secure and jealousy free, a person suffering from jealousy must break the habit of going into autopilot, by becoming more conscious of their thoughts and feelings that lead to jealousy.

Our Brain Is A Drug Factory

From a physiological point of view, jealousy is a chemical response to how we think and feel. Scientists have proved that our thoughts trigger the release of chemicals within our body. In fact, every single thought you will ever have throughout your entire life, will produce either good chemicals that make you feel positive or negative chemicals that make you feel bad. **Whenever we dwell upon positive thoughts such as love or happiness our brain produces a chemical called serotonin.** Serotonin is one of the chemicals artificially produced through the taking of antidepressant drugs, serotonin is what's known as the happy drug.

On the other end of the scale, whenever we dwell upon negative thoughts such as anger or jealousy our brain produces chemicals such as adrenaline and cortisol. This negative chemical adrenaline is the chemical that triggers our body's fight or flight response; it increases our heart rate and it also takes blood away from our important body parts such as our brain and gut, and diverts it to our muscles ready for immediate action if so needed. Cortisol is often referred to as the stress hormone, people who suffer from depression and chronic stress, normally have within their blood stream a very high level of this negative chemical.

Adrenaline and cortisol do have their uses, for instance; if you were in a jungle and you saw a lion pounding towards you with its mouth wide open, in such extreme circumstances adrenaline and cortisol would be essential for your survival. However, in a relationship setting where we need to think and act in a rational way, adrenaline and cortisol work against our best interests, by affecting our temperament in a negative way.

By being aware of these facts that our thoughts produce chemicals that make us feel positive or negative, we can choose which thoughts we choose to dwell upon. Throughout this book we will be focusing on how we can use our mind to get into good habits, to produce chemicals that make us feel positive and secure. **To be free from jealousy we must learn how to use our mind to its fullest potential.**

Are You Jealous?

Are you suffering from jealousy yourself? How do you know if you're suffering with jealousy? What are the symptoms of being jealous? If you are already suffering from jealousy, then the likelihood of you already being aware of your own insecurities may be the main reason why you are taking the time to read this book. **One of the easiest ways of knowing if you are suffering with jealousy is to become aware of your thought patterns, what are you thinking when you think of your partner?** What images are you creating inside your head? Are they images of your partner flirting with someone else? Do you see images of your partner in the arms of someone else? What's the little voice in your head saying? Does your internal voice say negative stuff about your partner to make you feel bad? The thoughts you create and dwell upon will be the deciding factor in whether you are suffering with jealousy or not.

If you're not certain that you are suffering with jealousy, below are some of the most common symptoms and signs.

Signs and symptoms of suffering from jealousy:

23

- Do you often ask where your partner is going?

- Do you worry that your partner will be unfaithful?

- Do you often question your partner's whereabouts if they turn up late?

- Do you feel uncomfortable whenever a man/woman talks to your partner?

- Do you check your partner's private messages?

- Do you feel the need to be around or in touch with your partner constantly?

- Have you ever had a partner accuse you of being jealous?

Can you relate to any of the symptoms above? If the answer is yes, then it's most likely that you are suffering from jealousy. Most people at some point during their life will suffer from jealousy, to some degree or another.

In the section **How To Stop Being Jealous**, you will learn the techniques of how to change your thoughts and feelings and how to overcome this destructive behaviour. Jealousy doesn't have to be a long-term problem that interferes with your day to day life. The good news is that with the help of this book, you can change your negative thought patterns and become jealousy free.

Is Your Partner Jealous?

How can you tell if your partner is suffering with jealousy? What are the telltale signs? In a new relationship it can be quite difficult at first to pick up on the signs that someone is suffering with jealousy, simply because when we are in a new relationship we always try to be on our best behaviour and only show our positive attributes. Most people who do suffer with jealousy are fully aware of their negative feelings and tend to suppress them as much as possible especially at the beginning of a relationship. However, over time jealousy becomes impossible to hide, and our true nature becomes quite apparent. The true indication that your partner is in fact suffering with jealousy will come about through your partner's behaviour. Your partner's behaviour will betray their jealous thoughts.

If you're still not certain that it is jealousy that your partner is suffering from, below are some of the most common symptoms and signs that will indicate that your partner is in fact suffering from jealousy.

Common telltale signs that your partner suffers with jealousy:

- Do you get a feeling that your partner doesn't trust you?

- Does your partner often ask where you are going?

- Does your partner often question your whereabouts, if you turn up late?

- Does your partner seem to be uncomfortable, whenever a man/woman talks to you?

- Have you ever found evidence that your partner has been snooping on your private messages?

- Has your partner ever admitted to being jealous?

Does your partner show any of these symptoms from the above? If the answer is yes, then your partner is suffering from jealousy. Jealousy is far more common than you may think, the section on **How To Help You Partner To Be Jealousy Free** will guide you through the process on how to help your partner become jealousy free, if they are ready and willing to be helped. This book is about how to have a great relationship without jealousy.

Fred & Jane, Susan & Dave

"Jealousy is, I think, the worst of all faults because it makes a victim of both parties."

Gene Tierney.

Throughout this book we will be coming into contact with our four leading characters. We have Fred who suffers with jealousy and his partner Jane who doesn't. We also have Dave and his partner Susan, who suffers with jealousy.

We will be following Fred and Susan's journey of self-discovery and their trials and errors in becoming free from jealousy. We will also be following Dave and Jane's journey in helping their partners to become jealousy free.

Fred & Jane's Story

Fred met his partner Jane at a Christmas work's party, Fred knew from the very first moment he set eyes on Jane, that she was the one for him. Jane on the other hand wasn't as keen.

However, over a period of six months Fred's persistence paid off and he finally won Jane's love.

At the beginning of the relationship Fred and Jane were extremely happy, Fred was the personification of everything Jane was looking for in a man, he was kind, thoughtful and loving, but after a few weeks into the relationship Jane noticed a change in Fred's personality; he was becoming more and more insecure and jealous as the weeks passed by.

Two months into Fred and Jane's relationship:

Fred says, *"Surely you're not wearing that skirt to go to the office party, are you?"*

Jane says, *"Yes I am, why, what's wrong with it?"*

Fred says, *"Don't you think it's a bit too short? "*

Jane says, *"No it's not, you always say it looks nice! Besides you bought it for me, and now all of a sudden, it's a bit short! "*

Fred says, *"I just thought that the party was more of a formal party, than a casual one, why don't you wear something else? "*

Jane says, *"There you go again, trying to tell me what I should and shouldn't wear. I'm sick and tired of all this."*

Susan & Dave's Story

Susan and Dave met online. Susan had been single for just over three months. Dave had been single for nearly a year. Susan and Dave had been chatting online for a few weeks until Dave eventually plucked up the courage to ask Susan on a date, and they have been dating ever since. Susan and Dave were so happy to begin with, they had so many things in common, they loved the same sort of music, and once a week they would go dancing at the local dance hall.

However, after a few weeks into the relationship, Dave started to notice that Susan was beginning to become far clingier and more possessive; it became apparent to Dave, that Susan was extremely jealous.

Five weeks into Susan and Dave's relationship;

Susan says, *"Why is it every time we go to the local supermarket, you always seem to go to that checkout, where that young woman is working?"*

Dave says, *"What young woman are you talking about?"*

Susan says, *"Don't pretend you don't know who I am talking about. The one with the false boobs, the one who's always fluttering her false eyelashes at you. You must think I'm stupid, I know you fancy her!"*

Dave says, *"I can't believe you're being like this again, I go to the checkout, with the least people in, not because of the person working it."*

Susan says, *"I don't know why you're with me, when you can't keep your eyes off other women, aren't I enough for you?"*

Dave says, *"I don't want to be with anyone else, I love you, why can't you believe me? I'm sick and tired of this all the time. I'm going for a walk."*

Jealousy in a relationship is like cancer, unless stopped and cut out, it spreads and devours anything that is good, until there is little left that is good and decent. With the help of this book you can learn to break free from the chains of jealousy.

Chapter 2

How To Be Jealousy Free

Genuine Concerns

You Are What You Think!

What's Your Why?

The Power Of Love

What You See Is What You Feel

What You Say, Affects How You Feel

The Magic Of Humour

Letting Go Of Your Fears

Letting Go Of The Past

Love Yourself First

Stop Comparing

Don't Believe Everything You Think!

Breaking The Trance

How To Be Jealousy Free

"The jealous are troublesome to others, but a torment to themselves."

William Penn.

Jealousy like any human negative behaviour is something that we have learned, and anything learned can be unlearned and a new positive behaviour adopted. By implementing the techniques that are outlined within this book, you can teach yourself to be jealousy free. Just by you merely taking the time to read this book you have already taken your first crucial step on your journey of becoming jealousy free. Reading a book on self-help takes great courage and fortitude, no one likes to change because change makes people feel uncomfortable. If you feel that you are ready and willing to make the changes that are necessary to lead you to a more secure and happier life, not only for yourself but for your loved ones also, then this book is for you.

Most people tend to just get through life the best way they can, instead of getting out of life the best they can. Most

35

people hope that one day their life will magically change for the better overnight, but life doesn't work that way. Whatever you want in life, whether to have the job of your dreams, or to rid yourself of a negative behaviour such as jealousy, you have to do something that most people won't do, which is to change ourselves.

Within this particular section, we will be looking at how you can free yourself of your jealous ways, and take back control of your own mind, by changing the way you think and feel about things, that in the past would have turned you green with jealousy.

A lot of the information we are going to address within this book is simple yet challenging. **Jealousy like any other deep-seated feeling, cannot be instantly changed overnight, sadly there is no magic wand.** However, take heart for as soon as you begin to think better, you will start to feel better, and by feeling better, you will also begin to feel more secure and less jealous.

This book will help you to become secure, confident and far less stressed. It will also give you the techniques for you to achieve your desired goal, in becoming jealousy free. There will be sections within this book that you may regard as not particularly relevant to your situation, or circumstance, however it's advisable to read through this entire section, to get the best from this book.

Remember you are the architect and director of your life. If you don't control your jealousy, your jealousy will control you.

Genuine Concerns

Before we get into the methods and techniques of how to be jealousy free, it would be naive of us not to explore the possibility that your feelings of insecurity and jealousy are not based on genuine, legitimate concerns. If after all it turns out that your partner is in fact a lying cheating love rat, who's sleeping with your best friend, then no amount of self-change, will alter the situation.

So, what would constitute a genuine, legitimate concern that needs to be addressed? A genuine legitimate concern can be anything from a sudden change in your partner's behaviour, to an unfamiliar shift in your partner's character.

Examples of some legitimate concerns that need further explanation:

- A sudden change in your partner's personality?

- A sudden change to your partner's routine?

- A sudden change in your sex life?

- Has your partner suddenly become secretive with their phone or computer?

- Have you found physical signs; aftershave/lipstick marks that make you suspicious?

If you have found that your partner's character and behaviour has suddenly changed or if you find unusual physical evidence, such as lipstick on the collar or aftershave on their clothing, THEN YOU DO HAVE A GENUINE REASON TO BE CONCERNED, AND YOU DO HAVE A RIGHT TO ASK YOUR PARTNER, FOR AN EXPLANATION. Remember though, having a genuine reason to be concerned doesn't give you, an excuse to throw wild accusations about, or have their bags packed ready for them, as soon as they walk through the door. It's important to remember that two plus two, doesn't equal five. Just because your partner's behaviour or character changes doesn't mean that they are up to no good. Your partner may have a genuine, legitimate, and innocent reason for your concerns.

Let's say for instance that you notice that your partner is suddenly becoming more secretive with their mobile phone. What does that mean? Does it mean that your partner has a secret lover and is being unfaithful? Does it mean that your partner is planning to leave you? Or is it because it's your birthday next month, and your partner is planning a secret birthday surprise for you? Who knows?

The only person who does know for sure is your partner, and without you knowing the real reason, your mind will just go on presuming the worst reason.

Dealing With Legitimate Concerns

The best way to deal with a legitimate concern is to be direct with your partner, and to simply ask them the reasons behind the changes. Ask in a matter of a fact way, without any negative accusations. If you find that your partner doesn't want to discuss it for whatever reason, be persistent until you get an explanation.

Your partner may have a perfectly good reason for their sudden change in character or behaviour. It is therefore important not to jump to conclusions, as soon as you notice something out of place. Ask the question!

Ask the question:

- Why aren't we talking like we used to?

- Why all of a sudden are you behaving differently?

- Why don't you want to make love?

- Why have you all of a sudden put a passcode on your phone?

- Why is there lipstick on your collar?

Unless you raise the subject directly with your partner, a mind prone to jealousy will run wild, and before you know it your imagination will have your partner sleeping with everyone, including your best friend. The mind generally creates a situation that is entirely negative, and as far from reality as possible.

Fred says, *"Why is it, suddenly within the last week or so, you've had to work over so often?"*

Jane says, *"Oh I've been meaning to tell you, the boss has been off sick all week with the flu, I'm shattered."*

Nine times out of ten your partner will want to elevate your concerns and worries, however if you find your partner defensive or unhelpful, then you have no choice but to insist for an explanation, for your own peace of mind, and your partner's.

Genuine Concerns

1. Genuine, legitimate concerns need to be addressed.

2. A genuine concern could be a sudden change in your partner's character, behaviour or unusual physical evidence that you may find.

3. Don't jump to conclusions, your partner may have a legitimate and innocent reason for your concerns.

4. Be direct with your partner and simply ask them the reasons behind the changes, in a matter of a fact way, without any negative accusations.

You Are What You Think!

"Jealousy lives upon doubts. It becomes madness or ceases entirely as soon as we pass from doubt to certainty."

Francois de La Rochefoucauld.

What is it that makes you jealous? Is it down to your genetic makeup? Because of something that happened in the past or is it because of your partner's behaviour? No, it has nothing to do with your genetic makeup, and it's not because of whatever happened in your past, or the way that your partner behaves now. The reason why you suffer with jealousy is because of the way you THINK. You make yourself feel jealous because of the negative images you create, and the negative thoughts you allow to manifest in your mind. JEALOUSY IS SUBJECTIVE, NOT OBJECTIVE. No one, including your partner, can make you feel jealous. Just like no one can make you feel happy. Happiness comes from within. The way that you feel and the way that you behave, are a result of how you choose to think.

Your feelings and behaviour are but mere reflections of your thoughts.

Fred says, *"Jane makes me feel so jealous!"*

Fred is wrong, the truth of the matter is Jane nor anyone else on the planet, can make Fred feel anything, including jealousy. Fred makes himself feel jealous. People who suffer with jealousy don't think jealous thoughts because they are jealous, they are jealous, because they think jealous thoughts.

It's only when you take responsibility for your own thoughts and feelings, that you can begin to change your jealous behaviour. Once you begin to accept responsibility for that, you can then begin the process of change within yourself that will lead you to freedom.

Let's take a look at a couple of scenarios and see how people think differently, and therefore feel differently;

Scenario 1:

Susan and Jane are both attending their partner's work's Christmas party. During the evening, Susan and Jane both happen to see their partner laughing and in deep conversation with an attractive young work colleague.

Susan thinks, *"Who's she? She's very pretty. Dave seems to find her very entertaining, no wonder he can't wait to get to work in the mornings. He thinks, I'm stupid, I knew something was going on."*

Jane thinks, *"I'm so glad Fred is getting on well with the people he's working with, perhaps he may even get the promotion he applied for. Then we can think about getting the new holiday home by the coast that we've been talking about for so long. I do love him so much, he works so hard, I'm so lucky."*

Scenario 2:

Jane and Susan are both taking a call on their mobile phones. Whilst talking on the phone, they are both smiling and laughing. It soon becomes apparent that Jane and Susan are talking to their ex-partners.

Fred thinks, *"Jane always seems happy when her ex-partner phones, in fact even happier than when she's talking to me. I know she still loves him deep down."*

Dave thinks, *"I hope one day I can forgive my ex-partner the way Susan has forgiven hers, for the way he treated her. She's my inspiration in life."*

In both scenarios the circumstances are the same. So how can it be that two people, who experience, the same situation, can think and feel so differently?

The answer is simple, it's because Dave thinks differently to the way Fred thinks, and Jane, thinks differently to the way Susan thinks. The circumstances don't change, the only difference is the way that different people think.

Jealousy is created inside our own head; we make ourselves feel jealous and no one else is responsible. To be free from jealousy we must learn to accept this fact, instead of shifting the blame onto someone else. Once we have accepted this premise, we can then begin to change our thoughts and feelings.

To be jealousy free you must first take responsibility for your feelings and behaviour. You are the architecture of your life. Your happiness, security and peace of mind rests solely in your own hands, through the way you choose to think. **Taking responsibility for your jealous feelings is fundamental for you to succeed in being jealousy free.**

You Are What You Think

1. The reason why you are jealous is because of the way you think.

2. You make yourself jealous.

3. No one can make you feel jealous.

4. Your feelings and behaviour are but mere reflections of your thoughts.

5. To be jealousy free you must first take responsibility for your feelings and behaviour.

What's Your Why?

"It is not love that is blind, but jealousy."
Lawrence Durrell.

Why do you want to become jealousy free? What's your incentive? What's your why? Your why's are your incentives, the reasons for why you want to change. Your why is that driving force within you, that's prompting you to read this book.

Your why will be the determining factor in either your success or failure in becoming jealousy free. The stronger you make your why, (your incentive) the easier it will be for you to become jealousy free, however if your why is weak and undefined, the harder it will be to succeed.

Ask yourself, why do you want to be jealousy free.

What is your why?

- Is it because you want to be less stressed?

- Is it because you want to have a better relationship?

- Is it because you want to be happier?

- Is it because you want to make your partner happier?

Once you have thought about your why's, write them down. Get them out of your head and jot them down on paper in black and white. Look at them, study them and contemplate on your reasons and incentives for becoming jealousy free.

Susan says, *"If I wasn't jealous, I wouldn't be stressed every time Dave was late, I wouldn't be thinking that he was probably going to leave me for someone else.*
If I wasn't jealous, I would be much more relaxed, calm and peaceful. I would be so much happier; I don't think I would have so many headaches.
I know for sure; Dave would be happier if I was more secure and less stressed."

Susan knows exactly what her why's are, she knows that being jealousy free would change her life for the better and the positive effects it would have on her relationship with her partner.

Fred says, *"If I didn't suffer with jealousy, I suppose my partner would be happier. It's hard to think how things would be different. I don't know."*

In this example Fred's struggling to see the benefits of becoming jealousy free. He can't seem to find his why's and if Fred doesn't know why he wants to be jealousy free, then where is the incentive for him to change!

The Power Of The Imagination

"Remember that your imagination is yours and yours alone. You have the inborn capacity to use it in any way that you choose. No one else is responsible for your imagination. Anything placed in your imagination and held there ultimately becomes your reality."

Wayne Dyer.

If you are struggling to find your why, then you can use the power of your unconscious mind to show you what your incentives are in becoming free from jealousy.

Albert Einstein said *"Imagination is everything. It is the preview of life's coming attractions."* The power of the imagination is awesome, it is the creative force of the universe. Everything within the universe that is created, from the clothes that you wear, to the bed you sleep in, was first created within the mind, through the power of the imagination. In fact, everything that has been created and will be created, is but a pale reflection of the original, that resides within the mind of the creator. Albert Einstein also said, *"Logic will get you from A to B. Imagination will take you everywhere."* Einstein learned early on in his life, how to harness the great power of his unconscious mind, through the medium of the imagination. It was through the imagination, that Einstein came up with the theory of relativity, by using the power of the imagination he saw himself riding on a photon of light. The imagination works mainly through the medium of images, sounds and feelings. Just like Einstein, you too can use the power of your imagination to unlock the greater potential of your mind, to help you to become jealousy free.

It's not well known that our unconscious mind cannot distinguish between reality and imagination, therefore we can put this into practice by imagining ourselves the way we want to be, until it becomes our reality.

Practice this technique, close your eyes and imagine what your life would be like if you weren't suffering with jealousy. Use all your senses to make it feel as real as possible.

Ask yourself these questions:

- How would you feel different?

- How would you know if you weren't jealous?

- How would it make you feel if you were secure, and jealousy free?

- How would it change you?

- How would your partner be affected?

- Would you feel happier?

- Would your partner be happier?

Try to see all the details in your imagination: the images, the sounds and most importantly the feelings that go with them. Imagine how your relationship with yourself would be different and how your relationship with your partner would also change.

Once you can see and feel the benefits of becoming jealousy free in your mind's eye, open your eyes. Repeat this exercise at least once a day, ideally when you can relax either in the morning or in the evening before you go to sleep. With each time try to increase the detail, making the visualisation stronger and by increasing the details you will also be increasing your positive feelings that go along with the images.

The objective of this exercise is to get your unconscious mind into the habit of seeing yourself and your relationship in a new light. By doing so, you are training your unconscious mind to see and to feel yourself, in a new way. **A new you, who thinks, feels and behaves differently.**

Whenever you change your thoughts you are in effect physically changing your brain. Scientists say that by merely using your imagination, you are in fact physically creating new neural pathways and new connections within your brain which through repetition these pathways will get stronger and stronger, allowing your brain to function in a new positive way of thinking.

By using the power of your imagination, it is possible to realise your full potential. Imagining allows you to see the possibilities of what lay ahead and what you can achieve. This exercise will encourage a positive perspective on your current situation.

If you can make it real in your mind, then you can make it real on the outside. Finding your WHY will give the incentive and determination to make the changes in you. Imagine the way you want to be, until you become the way you imagine.

What's Your Why?

1. What's your incentive to become jealousy free?

2. Your why will be the determining factor in either your success or failure in becoming jealousy free.

3. Use the power of your imagination to see the possibilities of what you want in life.

4. If you can make it real in your mind, you can make it real on the outside.

The Power Of Love

"The love of liberty is the love of others; the love of power is the love of ourselves."

William Hazlitt.

T he power of love, sounds like a title of a book, the lyrics of a song, or the title from a religious sermon, however the power of love is the key to becoming jealousy free. It's been said that the power of love is the most powerful force in the universe. Religious leaders have spoken about the power of love for thousands of years. Some people say that's stupid! Yet essentially, nearly everything we do as a species, we do because of the two fundamental emotions that rule our life, FEAR and LOVE.

We wear the clothes that we love to wear. We watch the movies that we love to see. We eat the food that we love to eat. It is love that motivates and inspires us, and it is through this power of love that motivates the gardener to tend and cultivate his garden, come rain or shine. It is love that inspires the budding musician to spend hundreds and thousands of hours of practising, just to be able to play an instrument.

Make a list of ten things that you love and prioritise them, starting with what you love the most. That could be anything from your partner, to your shiny new car.

Let's take a look at Susan's list;

1. Friends.

2. Patrick Swayze.

3. Tigger the Cat.

4. Shoes.

5. Dave.

6. Chinese food.

7. The Jungle Book.

8. Walks by the sea.

9. Wine.

10. A massage.

Your list will give you an indication of where you see your love for your partner. In Susan's list, her partner Dave is fifth on the list, which is below Tigger the cat. Where is your partner on your list of importance and priorities? If your partner is not in your top three, then you will struggle to give your partner your best and therefore you will struggle to make the changes that are necessary to become free from jealousy.

Like everything else in your life, you will only get out, what you put in. For it will be the amount of love that you feel for your partner, that will finally be the deciding factor in whether you will be successful or not. In life we can only appreciate the things that we truly value.

Make Your Partner a Priority

If you find that your partner is not in your top three of the things you love the most, then you will have to change the way you see your partner. Your partner must become a priority, so that you can make the changes within yourself.

Begin by asking yourself these three fundamental questions:

- Why do you love your partner?

- What makes your partner so special to you?

- What would you miss the most, if your partner wasn't in your life?

To become secure in your relationship you must use the power of love for your partner, to help you overcome your insecure, jealous ways.

Write a list of at least ten things that you love about your partner. Start every sentence with the words, I love.

Ten things Susan loves about Dave:

1. I love the way he makes me feel about myself.

2. I love his sense of humour; he makes me laugh so much.

3. I love how he believes in me; he makes me feel confident.

4. I love the way he always puts me first, before anyone else.

5. I love the way he talks to me; he makes me feel special.

6. I love his sense of adventure; he makes me feel alive.

7. I love the way he holds and touches me.

8. I love the way he is in touch with his feelings.

9. I love how different he is to my ex-partner.

10. I love how spontaneous he is, he makes me feel young again.

The objective of this exercise is for you to know in your own mind, without a shadow of a doubt, the reasons why you love your partner. Specifically, what makes your partner so special? If for instance one of the reasons why you love your partner is because of how they make you feel, then list what those feelings are.

Once you have established within your own mind, why your partner is so special and precious to you, it will give you the incentive and the stamina to help you achieve your goal of being secure and jealousy free.

You have to get to the stage within your own mind, where your partner is in the top three of the things you love the most. When you move your partners position of importance within your own mind, you will then be able to make the changes within yourself. The more you value your partner for who they are, the easier it will be for you to change.

In life we have to look at our blessings, to secure our future.

The Power Of Love

1. Love and fear are the two fundamental emotions that rule our life.

2. What do you love? Make a list of ten things that you love the most.

3. If your partner is not in your top three of the things you love the most you will struggle to make the changes that are necessary to become free from jealousy.

4. Make your partner a priority.

5. The more you value your partner for who they are, the easier it will be for you to change your jealous ways.

What You See, Is What You Feel

How would you feel if someone showed you a photo or a video of your partner, with another person in a romantic setting? It's more than likely you would feel upset and angry, yet this is exactly how we choose to torture ourselves, day in day out, when we are insecure and jealous. At the time of writing this book, the 2017 horror film "*IT*", based on the Stephen King book, was being released in the cinema. The film revolves around a scary looking clown who feeds on people's fears. Since its release, it has petrified thousands, if not millions of people. (Some people not only like to feel scared they actually pay good money to be petrified.) In the 1982 classic block buster film "*E.T.*" co-produced and directed by Steven Spielberg, the world was introduced to the adorable creature "*E.T.*". In the film, this strange yet cute extra-terrestrial, crashes to Earth and is befriended by a young boy, who makes it his mission to help the creature get back home. The film "*E.T.*" has melted the hearts of millions, if not billions, of people, since it was released. **Hollywood is fully**

aware of the power of what we see, and how it affects how we feel. Yet the greatest theatre, is inside our own head, the movies of our mind. We have a choice to see images that make us feel good, or images that make us feel bad, the choice is ours.

The mind mainly thinks in images and it's the images that we create and choose to focus upon in our head that are the deciding factor in how we feel. Your unconscious mind cannot distinguish between a positive image and a negative image, to your unconscious mind an image is just an image. Whenever you think of something, your unconscious mind automatically converts your thoughts into images that you see within your mind's eye. Close your eyes and think of a huge, hairy spider walking towards you. What happened? You more than likely saw an image in your mind's eye, of a huge, hairy spider walking towards you, and truth be known you probably felt a bit scared. Close your eyes again, however this time think about being on an exotic beach somewhere enjoying yourself. What happened? You more than likely saw an image of yourself soaking up the sun rays, drinking a cocktail and having fun, plus you probably felt good because you were focusing upon a positive image.

If you think positively about your partner, you will see positive images of your partner, in your mind's eye, and you will feel positive about them. If you think negatively about your partner, you will see negative images of your partner, in your mind's eye, and you will feel negative about them.

Negative Images, Negative Feelings

Fred says, *"Whenever I think about Jane being at work, I get angry. Because in my mind, I see her flirting with other men. I know it sounds crazy, but I can't help how I feel."*

Why is Fred angry? Fred is angry because he is showing himself, (in his mind's eye) images of his partner Jane, flirting with other men. **Remember, whenever we think about something, our mind instantly changes those thoughts into images.** Close your eyes and think of something negative that makes you feel sad or annoyed. It could be something from a past event, or it could be something that's happening now in your life. Maybe it's someone who has offended you recently or perhaps it's someone who drives you nuts at work. Whichever memory you pick, see the image, or images in your mind's eye and focus on them. Imagine that you are in that moment right now, seeing what you saw, hearing what you heard and feeling how you felt. Now open your eyes. How do you feel? Do you feel a little upset or annoyed? If you created the images with enough clarity and realism, then you are more than likely feeling slightly negative in some way.

Positive Images, Positive Feelings

Dave says, *"Susan makes me happy; she makes me laugh so much. When I think about Susan, I think about the first time we met, I knew straight away, that she was the one for me. She's got beautiful eyes and a dirty laugh."*

Why is Dave so happy? Dave is happy because he is showing himself (in his mind's eye) images of Susan that make him feel happy and good.

Close your eyes again, but this time think of something that makes you feel happy and good. It could be a memory of when you achieved something special that you are proud of, such as when you passed your driving test, or it could be a memory from when you were a child. Again, whatever the memory is, see the image in your mind's eye as clear as possible, imagine that you are in that moment right now seeing what you saw, hearing the sounds that you heard and feeling all those good, happy feelings. Now open your eyes. How do you feel? Do you feel any different? Do you feel happier and more positive?

Why does it affect the way we feel when our mind conjures up positive or negative images? We feel differently because of the emotions and the feelings that are intertwined with those images. **Our unconscious mind cannot distinguish between what's real and what's not.** When you focus on images that have strong feelings connected to them, your brain produces the corresponding chemicals, that either make you feel good, by releasing the chemical serotonin, or by releasing the chemical cortisol to make you feel bad.

Change The Images

What images are you showing yourself over and over again in your head to make you feel so insecure and jealous? Are they negative or positive? To become jealousy free, you have to train your mind to focus on images that help you to feel positive and secure, images that will help you to feel good.

So how do you focus upon positive images that make you feel good and secure instead of focusing on negative images that make you feel bad and insecure. You do that by changing the dynamics of the images that you create in your mind that make you feel insecure and jealous, by replacing them with images that are more positive you will feel more secure.

If you change the way you look at things, the things you look at will change the way you feel. **You don't think jealous thoughts because you are jealous. You are jealous, because you think jealous thoughts.**

The next time you start to feel insecure and jealous, try to become aware of the images you are showing to yourself in your mind's eye that are making you feel so insecure and jealous. It may help to close your eyes so that you can focus and find that particular negative image that makes you feel jealous. Once you have found the negative image in your mind's eye, close your eyes and begin to imagine that all the colours in that image are draining away, until all that is left is a black and white image. Now imagine that you have a giant whiteboard eraser, like the ones that teachers use at school, and begin to rub out the image that you turned black and white, until there's nothing left of it.

Where the image that made you feel insecure and jealous once was, begin now to form a new image in your mind's eye. An image that makes you feel positive and secure. Enlarge the image until it becomes life size and add colour to it. The bigger and the more colourful you make your new positive image, the stronger your positive feelings will become.

Susan using the technique to change her images:

Dave has gone out for the evening with his friends. Susan's at home reading a book, when all of a sudden Susan starts to feel uncomfortable. She's thinking about Dave and what he may be getting up to. Within a matter of seconds, she's becoming anxious, she's got knots in her stomach and a banging headache.

Susan closes her eyes and searches for the negative image that's tormenting her, *"I can see Dave with his friend Tom at the bar, there are two pretty young women with them, they are talking and laughing together. Dave's flirting. I can always tell when Dave's flirting because he goes red in the cheeks."*

1. Susan finds the negative image that's making her feel so jealous and begins to drain all the colour and life from it, turning it black and white.

2. She then begins to rub out the black and white image, until there's nothing left to see.

3. She then forms a new larger and more positive image full of colour and life that makes her feel positive and secure.

Susan says, *"In the new image that I've created, I can now see Dave just enjoying himself, playing pool with his friends."*

Soon after Susan changed the images that made her feel so insecure and jealous to a more positive image that made her feel secure, her stomach stopped churning and her headache disappeared allowing her to finish her book.

When you dilute and erase negative images, that make you feel insecure and jealous, you are inadvertently also erasing the negative thoughts and feelings that go along with them. To be jealousy free you must take control of your thoughts or your thoughts will take control of you. **You must train your mind to see positive images of your partner and challenge and change the negative images that make you feel jealous.** Whenever you see images that make you feel bad, change it to a positive image that will make you feel good.

What You See Is What You Get

1. Your thoughts and the images that you choose to focus upon create your feelings.

2. If you think positively about your partner, you will see positive images that will make you feel positive. If you think negatively about your partner, you will see negative images that will make you feel negative.

3. To become jealousy free, you have to train your mind to focus on images that help you to feel positive and secure.

4. Whenever you see images that make you feel bad, change them to a positive image that will make you feel good.

What You Say, Affects How You Feel

How would you feel if someone said to you; *"You're not good enough for your partner, you're too fat."* Or *"Your partner doesn't love you; they still love their ex-partner."* Chances are you would more than likely feel upset and angry, yet this is another way people who suffer with jealousy tend to torture themselves. Just like the images we show ourselves in our head affect how we feel, what we say to ourselves also influences how we feel. How we talk to other people is important, but nowhere near as important as how we talk to ourselves. **Our mind can be our best friend, or our worst enemy.**

Fred is at the bank with his partner Jane, a man approaches and kisses Jane on the cheek, they start chatting about how good it is to see each other after such a long time.

Meanwhile, poor old Fred's blood is starting to boil, he's got steam coming out his ears and his heart is pumping ten to the dozen. Fred is turning into the green-eyed monster.

What's going on with Fred to make him feel so bad? Let's take a listen to Fred's internal voice:

Fred's internal voice, *"Who the hell is this man kissing my partner? How dare he. Why is she talking to him? I don't know him! How can she embarrass me like this? I can't believe this."*

As we can see from this example, it wasn't Fred's internal images this time that made him feel insecure and jealous. The culprit was in fact Fred's internal voice.

For some people who suffer with jealousy, it's not what they see inside their head that makes them feel insecure and jealous, it's what they hear inside their head that makes them feel so bad.

In the 1991 comedy film, *"Drop Dead Fred,"* Rik Mayall plays the character Fred who is an imaginary, mischievous companion to a little girl named Elizabeth. In the film, Fred is invisible to everyone else apart from Elizabeth and wherever Elizabeth goes, Fred goes too, causing mayhem and destruction. Because Fred was invisible to everyone else, it was poor Elizabeth who always got the blame.

The little voice inside our head, can at times be compared to this mischievous character "Drop Dead Fred" who loves to whisper negative things causing us to feel insecure and jealous. In this section, you are going to learn how to control your internal jealous voice, so that you can make the changes that will turn negative thinking to positive thinking. **We can either learn how to control our mind in a positive way or** we can let our mind be unbridled and control us in a negative way.

Recognising Your Internal Jealous Voice

The first step to changing your jealous internal voice, is being able to recognise it in the first place. You have to learn how to identify your own particular internal jealous voice, so that as soon as it begins to make you feel jealous you can spot it instantly. What does your "Drop Dead Fred" voice sound like? Does it speak louder than your normal internal voice? Does it speak quicker than your normal voice? Does it use abusive words? How does it differ from your normal internal voice? Become familiar with it so that you can learn how to recognise it.

Changing The Sound

Once you have learned how to distinguish your jealous internal voice, you can then begin the next step in how to change it. At the time of writing this book, Elvis Presley has been dead some forty odd years however, the voice of Elvis is still as popular today as it ever was. The power of his voice alone still sells millions of records every year. What we hear affects how we feel. The sound of a funny voice can make us laugh, a voice that sounds annoying, can annoy us. We all have that one friend, relative or work colleague that has a really annoying voice, the sort of voice that is so annoying, that as soon as you see that particular person, you hope that the floor will swallow you up.

According to some communication experts, the sound of our voice has more power than the words that we speak, they reckon that 55% of communication is through body language alone, a massive 38% is through the tone of voice, and only 7% of communication is actually in the words that are spoken. That means just by changing the tonality of our voice, we can have a major overall effect on communication and how we feel.

A great way to change your internal jealous voice, is to alter the sound of it in your head. Begin by picking a new internal voice, a voice that is unusual, perhaps a voice that is a bit strange or even a voice that makes you laugh when you hear it. The voice can belong to anyone or anything, from your mother-in-law, to a cartoon character like Bugs Bunny. It doesn't matter whom the voice belongs to, as long as it's a voice that is so unusual and unique, that you can instantly bring it to mind.

Once you have decided on a voice that you can instantly remember, close your eyes and imagine that you can hear the new voice as clear as if it were coming from right behind you. Fix the sound of that new voice firmly within your mind, ready for action. The next step is to change your old internal jealous voice to your new weird, funny voice as soon as it begins to torment you.

Now imagine the same scenario as before; Fred is at the bank with his partner, a man approaches and kisses Jane on the cheek, they start chatting about how good it is to see each other after such a long time. However, this time Fred smiles and waits to be introduced.

What's going on with Fred, why is he feeling so different? It's exactly the same situation, although a totally different outcome. What's happening inside Fred's head to make him feel not only ok, but to actually smile in exactly the same situation:

Fred's new internal voice, *"EH, WHAT'S UP DOC? EH WHAT'S THIS DUDE DOING KISSING MY GIRL, EH."*

Just by Fred changing his internal jealous voice into a silly Bugs Bunny voice, Fred found it almost impossible to become insecure and jealous. Fred was not only able to manage his jealous behaviour, he also felt calm and in control.

Find yourself a new internal voice that will make you feel good, and ditch your old negative, insecure voice. **When something sounds stupid and silly it's hard to get annoyed.** After a while, your negative "Drop Dead Fred" voice will eventually disappear.

Facts

Another great technique that you can use to change your internal jealous voice as it begins to bombard you with negative feelings is to simply challenge it with irrefutable facts.

Susan's partner Dave is over forty minutes late from work, Susan begins to feel uncomfortable, she begins to clock watch. Her stomach is in knots, she can feel a migraine coming on.

What's going on inside Susan's head to make her feel so bad?

Susan's internal voice, *"Why hasn't he phoned? I knew he was probably up to no good. I bet he's with one of those young hussies at work. The rat! I knew I shouldn't have trusted him."*

When Dave eventually arrives home from work, the house is full of smoke. For nearly an hour Susan has been listening to her jealous internal voice, filling her head with all the worst possible scenarios. Her blood pressure is sky high and she's got a terrible migraine. And to top it all off, Susan had forgotten to take the dinner out of the oven. Susan and Dave end up arguing for the rest of the night.

Ignorance cannot reside where knowledge lives. If your jealous internal voice is spouting wild accusations, a quick fact check can prevent a lot of pain. As soon as your jealous voice begins to torment you with negative comments, interrupt it straight away and begin to challenge those wild accusations.

Imagine the same scenario as before; Dave is over forty minutes late from work: Susan looks at the clock and decides to turn down the gas on the oven. She picks up the book she's been hoping to finish and begins to read it. After a short while Dave arrives home.

Dave walks through the door and says, *"Hi, honey, sorry I'm late, there was a terrible accident on the motorway. Dinner smells great."*

What's going on inside Susan's head to make her feel ok? It's the same situation, although a totally different outcome. What's different? Susan challenged her jealous voice with facts.

Susan's internal voice, *"Why hasn't he phoned? I knew...* Susan begins to be aware of her negative jealous voice and chooses to interrupt it with a positive one... *"Perhaps he's had to work over, or the traffic is heavy. I'm a bit concerned but I'll ask him when he gets home."*

By simply challenging and correcting her negative internal voice, Susan was able to relax herself and take control of her thoughts and her feelings. Her blood pressure would have begun to go back to normal and she would have prevented herself from suffering a migraine. Susan also got to finish her book and when Dave did arrive home, they enjoyed a lovely dinner together.

So, the next time your jealous internal voice starts to make you feel insecure and jealous, try to challenge the voice with facts and other possibilities.

When you control your thoughts, your thoughts can't control you.

Pattern Interrupt

Another powerful method to stop your internal voice making you feel jealous is a technique used in NLP (Neuro Linguistic Programming) called pattern interrupt. Pattern interrupt can be used in various situations to rapidly change a thought pattern or behaviour.

A scuffle breaks out at a school, there's pandemonium, there's pushing, shoving, shouting and screaming, until all of a sudden, a teacher materialises from nowhere like a magician, shouting "STOP" at the top of his voice. Within seconds the skirmish is over, the children scatter just as fast as the teacher appeared.

The teacher's course of action causes enough confusion within the minds of the combatants to stop the fight. The action taken by the teacher is a classic example of a **pattern interrupt.** The great thing about this technique is that you can use it to combat and defeat your own jealous internal voice.

The next time your jealous internal voice starts to whisper negative stuff into your ear, just say STOP! It's best to say it out loud, if however, you are somewhere where it would be inappropriate to just blurt out the word STOP then say the word STOP under your breath. By the mere act of telling your jealous internal voice to STOP, you are interrupting the flow of your jealous thoughts and training your mind to not dwell upon negative thoughts. Just say STOP!

What You Say, Affects How You Feel

1. What you SAY to yourself also affects how you FEEL.

2. For some people who suffer with jealousy, it's not what they see inside their head that makes them feel insecure and jealous, it's what they hear.

3. A great way to change your internal jealous voice, is to alter the sound of it in your head.

4. If your jealous internal voice is spouting wild accusations, a quick fact check can prevent a lot of pain.

5. Pattern interrupt. The next time your jealous internal voice starts to whisper negative stuff into your ear, just say STOP!

The Magic Of Humour

There is a lot of truth in the old saying *"Laughter is the best medicine."* Whenever we laugh our brain releases positive chemicals into our body that make us feel happy and relaxed. These positive chemicals called endorphins, are opposites to the chemicals that are released when we are angry or jealous. **The more we laugh the better we will feel.**

The year was 1940, it was a year the world held its breath as the Nazis swept through Europe. During that year, Charlie Chaplin released and starred in the film, *The Great Dictator* wherein Chaplin played the part of a mad Dictator who wanted to take over the world. In this film, Chaplin used the medium of laughter to show the world the true horrors and dangers of fascism.

In the classic Monty Python's film *Life of Brian,* Graham Chapman plays the part of Brian Cohen, who unfortunately for him, gets mistaken for Jesus Christ, and is consequently arrested and executed (it really is a comedy.) However, towards the end of the film as Brian's life was ebbing away upon the cross, the followers of Jesus began to sing the now, notorious song, "Always look on the bright side of side of life. *Life of Brian* brilliantly highlights that no matter the circumstances we may find ourselves in, humour can always help to alleviate our pain.

How can humour help with jealousy? When we have humour in our lives, we feel happy and relaxed and when we feel happy and relaxed it's almost impossible to become insecure and jealous. When you choose to see things from a humorous point of view, life will always be that little bit easier for you to cope with.

Can you imagine for a moment what your life would be like if you had the ability to see the world through the eyes of a comedic legend, such as Stan Laurel or Rowan Atkinson and see how they choose to see the world. **By choosing to see the world and the people around you in a less serious light, it then becomes almost impossible for you to become insecure and jealous.**

We should all learn to laugh more, instead of taking life so seriously. By making time for humour within your life, you are in effect making time for happiness. And where happiness resides jealousy cannot. Always look on the brighter side of life. Turn your face towards the sun and the shadows will fall behind you. What or who, makes you laugh? When was the last time you had a real belly laugh?

The Magic Of Humour

1. When we laugh our brain releases positive chemicals, into our body that make us feel happy and relaxed.

2. When we are happy and relaxed it's almost impossible to become insecure and jealous.

3. The more you laugh the better you will feel.

Letting Go Of Your Fears

"I have lived through some terrible things in my life, some of which actually happened."
Mark Twain.

Do you know what it is that people fear the most? It's not the fear of spiders or even the fear of dying, it is the fear of speaking in public. It's hard to believe that most people would rather die or have a giant spider crawl on their face than speak in front of a group of people.

It's astonishing how fear controls so many people's lives. There are people who literally imprison themselves, in their own home because of fear. Some people never experience the thrill and excitement of flying to a new destination, because of the fear of flying. Fear stifles who we truly are and inhibits our potential.

Jealousy and fear go hand in hand; they're deeply entwined. For you to become free from jealousy, you must be bold and be prepared to address some of your deepest fears. What's strange about our fears, is that the great majority of what we actually fear, doesn't actually come to pass and the small percentage that does come to pass, normally turns out to be not as bad as we first imagined.

Our fears become a habit that dominate our thoughts and influence our behaviour.

What Do You Fear?

What do you fear? People who suffer with jealousy are swamped in fear. Fear that their partner will one day just up leave them. Fear that their partner will be unfaithful. Fear that they are not good enough for their partner.

To be free from jealousy you must be free from your fears that make you feel jealous. Take some time to write down your fears, putting them in black and white so that you can see them physically on the page in front of you. Having your fears on paper is a much better place than your fears being locked away in your head causing you and your loved one's confusion and misery.

Let's take a look at Susan's fears;

1. Being alone.

2. Rejection.

3. Not being loved.

4. To feel unattractive.

5. Not being accepted for who I am.

6. To be made to look like a fool.

7. To be betrayed.

Once you have written down your list, the next important step is to share them with your partner.

Sharing Your Fears

"The most difficult thing is the decision to act, the rest is merely tenacity. The fears are paper tigers. You can do anything you decide to do. You can act to change and control your life; and the procedure, the process is its own reward."

Amelia Earhart. "

Have you ever heard the expression; A problem shared is a problem halved? Well apparently, it's true. **According to studies from the university of Southern California Marshall School of Businesses, where researchers conducted experiments with people who were suffering from stress and fear. In their findings, they found that the people who did share their concerns and fears with other people, had considerably lower levels of stress within their body afterwards, than those people who kept their thoughts and feelings to themselves.** This study shows just by the mere act of sharing your concerns and fears with someone else, you can make yourself feel better, and who else better to share your fears and concerns with, than the person you love the most - your partner.

What happens if you don't choose to share your fears with your partner? Quite simply NOTHING happens, everything will stay the same. You will more than likely continue to be just as insecure and jealous as you were before, in fact your jealousy may even get worse and eventually you could end up separating. If you don't share your fears and concerns with your partner, then your partner won't be able to understand why you feel so insecure and jealous.

Susan says, *"Why do you have to be so friendly to that girl at the store? Every time we go there, you're all over her like a rash."*

Dave says, *"What are you talking about? I'm friendly most of time, with most people."*

Susan says, *"You must think I'm stupid, I know you want to sleep with her."*

How does Susan come across in that last statement, insecure, irrational? If Dave was aware of some of Susan's underlying fears, he would then perhaps be in a position to help her in some way or even at the very least understand WHY she is thinking in such an irrational way.

Keeping your fears to yourself when you suffer with jealousy is counterproductive, and quite frankly detrimental to not only yourself, but your partners health and happiness also. By sharing your fears, you're giving your partner an opportunity to stand in your shoes, even if those shoes are uncomfortable to wear at times. For a relationship to work you have to be honest and talk to your partner, share your concerns and fears with them, give them the chance and opportunity to take a glimpse into your internal world.

Now let's take a look at another scenario, Susan is being open and sharing some of her fears with her partner:

Susan says, *"I don't know why, but sometimes I think that you will just up and leave me one day, when you find someone younger and prettier. After all, who could blame you. I've let myself go; I hate the way I look. I don't know why you are with me."*

Dave says, *"I'm with you because I love you. You mean the world to me. To me you are beautiful, I adore you. I will never leave you."*

Susan says, *"You make me so happy. I'm sorry, I know you love me. Things are going to be different. I'm going to change."*

Admitting your fears and having the courage to share them with the person you love takes strength.

By sharing your fears with your partner, you are giving them the opportunity to help in some way, even if it is just being there for you. It doesn't matter how crazy or stupid you think your partner will think you are, if your partner does truly love and want to be with you, they will want to help you by alleviating your worries and fears. **Remember, getting help** shows strength, not weakness. Overcoming your fears, will help you to overcome your jealousy.

Letting Go Of Your Fears

1. To become free from jealousy, you must be bold and be prepared to address some of your deepest fears.

2. By sharing your fears with your partner, you are giving your partner the opportunity to help.

3. Getting help shows strength, not weakness.

Letting Go Of The Past

"There is no love without forgiveness, and there is no forgiveness, without love."

Bryant H. McGill.

Have you ever had a partner who cheated on you and broke your heart? Perhaps you've had a partner who lied and deceived you. Do you still feel hurt and angry? If the answer is yes, then it's highly likely you are struggling with letting go of the past. **To be successful in becoming jealousy free, you must learn how to be free from the hurt and pain of the past, so that you can move forward with your present life.**

Whenever a person betrays our trust, especially someone whom we once loved, that betrayal can at times feel like a knife thrust into our heart. And unless we can learn to move on from such hurt and betrayal, that bitterness and hatred will over time turn us into someone who is bitter and full of hate.

Holding onto hurt and anger is like trying to hold onto a burning ember, the longer we hold on to it, the worse we will feel.

Fred says, *"I will never forgive my ex-partner for running off with my best friend."*

The sad thing is, that Fred probably won't ever be able to forgive his ex-partner or his old friend whilst he chooses not to. Let's take a look at Fred's potential future, if he keeps to his word and chooses to never forgive his ex-partner and his so-called best friend, who will end up suffering the most? It will unfortunately be poor old Fred; in fact, the perpetrators of the affair will go throughout life virtually untouched by Fred's decision to not forgive them. Fred will be the one whose heart will beat faster than normal because of his negative thought patterns this will in turn produce negative chemicals, such as adrenaline and cortisol, therefore increasing the risk of heart complications in the future. These negative chemicals will also affect Fred's digestive system in such a way that Fred could end up with stomach ulcers, and possibly other unhealthy stress related problems due to his negative thought patterns. Over time, Fred's frame of mind and personality will become far more pessimistic and negative, his mind will turn bitter with hate and regret, and before Fred knows what's happened, he's turned into someone suffering from jealousy.

Forgiveness

How do you forgive someone who has broken your heart? You learn to forgive that person by first knowing the reason why you are choosing to forgive them, and that reason is first and foremost, for your own happiness and wellbeing. **When you choose to forgive someone who has hurt you, you don't forgive that person for their benefit, you forgive them for your benefit.** When you choose to forgive, you are choosing to do so, so that you may move on with your own life, so that you may be happy and secure in the here and now. Forgiving someone doesn't mean you agree, or even understand why that person did what they did. Forgiveness doesn't take away the pain of what they did, it just stops the pain from continuing throughout your life. **Forgiveness just means that you accept what's happened, so that you are able to move forward with your life in the here and now.**

There are very few cruel and nasty people in the world, however there are people who do cruel and stupid things sometimes. As soon as you make that choice to forgive the people who have hurt you, you will instantly start to feel mentally and physically better within yourself and when you feel better within yourself, your present and future relationships will also undoubtedly improve.

When you let go of the past, the past will let go of you.

Haunted

Fred says, *"Whenever I think of my previous relationship, the first thing that pops into my head, is the image of seeing my ex-partner in bed with my so-called best friend. If only I could erase that image out of my head, I know I wouldn't feel so messed up."*

Have you got a memory that haunts you? A memory of something you wish you could erase from your mind. Wouldn't it be great if we could just wipe all of our unpleasant memories from our mind? However, it was only a few decades ago that doctors tried to do just that, wipe people's minds. This highly controversial procedure was called a lobotomy. The surgeons would cut out pieces of brain matter in order to try and help people live better lives. The procedure was meant to alter the personality of the subject, towards a more productive life. Sadly, many of these procedures ended up causing far more complications and problems than they cured.

What about time travel, wouldn't it be great if we could travel back in time and just tweak circumstances to our advantage. Unfortunately, time travel hasn't been invented yet, so we can't travel back in time and there is no magic pill to erase certain negative memories from our mind. However, the one thing that we do have the power to change, is how we choose to see those memories in the here and now. Whenever we think of an event from our past, we have to resort to using our imagination, to hear and see those events as they were.

Our imagination recreates those past events through images and sounds. Our mind is like a home cinema, we can either see positive images that will make us feel good or negative images that make us feel bad. **Just by changing the images we focus upon; we change how we think and feel.**

Fool Your Mind

Andrew Matthews wrote in *Being Happy*! that to be happy we should *"Concentrate on and enjoy what you have. Don't dwell on losing what you have."*

One of the most fascinating aspects of your unconscious mind is the fact that it cannot tell the difference between reality and imagination. You can prove this fact to yourself by doing the 'Lemon Test.'

Sit or lay down somewhere quiet and comfy and close your eyes. Relax your body from the top of your head to the bottom of your feet and once you have achieved physical relaxation, imagine in your mind holding a lemon. Feel the weight of the lemon in your hand, feel the rough texture of the lemons skin. Study the bright colours of the lemon, see how it sparkles in the light. In your imagination, see yourself cutting the lemon in half and watching the juice cascading from the fruit, whilst inhaling the aroma. Now imagine taking a bite out of the lemon and tasting the bittersweet juice.

Now open your eyes. What happened? Could you feel and see the lemon in your mind's eye? Could you smell the juice as you cut through it? Could you taste the bittersweet flesh of the lemon? Did your mouth fill with saliva because of the bitterness of the fruit?

If the answer is yes, then you fooled your unconscious mind through the power of your imagination, and your body responded as if the lemon was real. Your unconscious mind was unable to tell the difference between a real lemon and a strongly imagined one. What's significant is the fact that your memories, GOOD and BAD are made up from IMAGES that you conjure up within your mind. So, if you have a memory that makes you feel bad, all you have to do is change that negative image that's linked to that particular memory, to a positive image that makes you feel good.

Change The Image

Ask yourself this, if you had a painting hanging in your living room that you detested, would you leave it there? Of course not, you would swap it for a painting that you loved, an image that made you feel good. This is the same as the images you hold in your mind, if you are going to look back at the past every now and then, you may as well look at things that make you feel happy and good.

To become free from a memory that haunts you, you have to change your internal negative images that make you feel bad, to images that makes you feel positive and good.

How to change a negative image, into a positive image:

To change a persistent negative image from your memory that haunts you, you must know exactly what that image is. What is it exactly that your unconscious mind conjures up to make you feel so bad? Close your eyes and think about that negative memory that you want to change. See that particular image in detail; who is in the image? What's happening?

Fred says, *"The memory that haunts me, is the image I see of my ex-partner, in bed with my best friend."*

Once you have found the specific image in your mind's eye that makes you feel bad, begin to look at the whole context that the negative image is set in: for instance, how big is the image in your mind? Is it a huge image? If so, how big? Is it a life size image? Is the image moving like in a cinema? Or is the image static? Is the image in colour or black and white? Is there any sound connected to the negative memory?

Fred says, *"It's a big image, it's bigger than me, it's about seven foot tall. The image isn't moving it's just like a poster, the image is in colour. There is a sound connected to the image, I can hear my footsteps as I'm walking up the stairs."*

Once you have all the specific details of the image, close your eyes once again and think about that memory that haunts you, see the image in your mind's eye however this time, you are going to change the dynamics of that particular negative memory through the power of your imagination. If there is colour in your image, begin by draining out all the colour, turning the image into a black and white image. Once you have done that, begin to shrink the image to the size of a book and if there is any sound to the negative memory, begin to turn it down until it becomes inaudible.

Fred says, *"Ok I have shrunken the image down, I've drained all the colour out turning it into a black and white image, and I've turned the sound off."*

Now that you have distorted the image of the negative memory that makes you feel bad, it's time to replace it with a new, positive image that will make you feel good. If your negative memory is to do with an ex-partner, then swap it for a positive image from that relationship. It could be an image of when you first met or perhaps a time when you did feel happy together. It doesn't really matter when, where or what the actual image is, as long as it's a positive image that you can easily remember and bring to mind.

The most important part of this process is to choose an image that you can easily remember, and an image that makes you feel good.

Fred says, *"Ok, I have chosen a positive image from when I first met my ex-partner. When we felt really happy together."*

Once you have decided on a new positive image, it's then time to swap the old image for the new one. Close your eyes

94

again and in your mind's eye, see the new positive image that makes you feel good and put it side by side with the old negative image that you have distorted. In your imagination, begin to see your new positive image growing in size, until it completely covers the old negative image, make your new positive image grow to the same size as your old negative image was or even bigger. Now add colour, depth, and sound to your new positive image, make it come alive, make it as real and vivid as possible.

Repeat this technique of changing the old negative image that makes you feel bad to a positive new image that makes you feel good once or twice a day for at least a week, preferably in the morning or evening when you are most relaxed. By repeating this exercise over and over again in your imagination, your brain is creating new stronger, more positive neural pathways making it easier for you to see the new positive image instead of the old negative image. After a week or so of doing these simple but powerful steps, your mind will automatically go to the new positive image and in doing so you will start to feel more positive and comfortable about that particular time in your life.

Fred says, *"Wow, I've swapped the old image that made me feel so bad, for an image that makes me feel good. I've been doing it for a few days now. It's so strange! Now whenever I do think of the past with my ex-partner, this new positive image automatically pops into my mind, instead of the old image that used to make me feel bad. I'm amazed it really works! I don't feel angry as much as I used to. I feel happier and more relaxed. It's like magic."*

Whenever we think back to a negative experience in our life our mind vividly conjures up what we heard, saw and felt. Because our unconscious mind cannot distinguish between what's real and what's not, it's as if we re-live the bad experience over and over again in our head. However, with this powerful technique you can change any negative memory that makes you feel bad and swap it with a new positive memory that makes you feel good. **This powerful life changing technique is not magic, but it can sometimes feel like magic.**

Letting Go Of The Past

1. Unless we can move on from hurt and betrayal, that bitterness and hatred will over time turn us into someone who is bitter and full of hate.

2. There are very few cruel and nasty people in the world, however there are people who do cruel and stupid things sometimes.

3. When you choose to forgive, you are choosing to do so, so that you may move on with your own life, so that you may be happy and secure in the here and now.

4. You can't change the past but what you can change is how you choose to see those memories in the here and now.

5. Just by changing the images you focus upon; you change how you think and feel.

Love Yourself First

"There is only one happiness in this life, to love and be loved."

George Sand.

Do you love yourself? Most people would say no, in fact most people struggle to even like themselves, especially people who suffer with jealousy. Yet to become jealousy free, self-love is essential. For it is only when we learn to love ourselves that we can truly love our partner.

Your happiness and love life depend solely and utterly upon the love that you have for yourself. Your outer world is simply a reflection of your inner world. If you treat yourself poorly, then you will more than likely treat your partner poorly. If you always put yourself down, then you more than likely put your partner down. If you don't love yourself, you won't be able to truly love your partner and if you don't love yourself, then how can you believe that someone else could love you?

Loving yourself is not about being vain or conceited, it is about accepting yourself for who you are with all your strengths, and faults. It is about liking yourself for the person you have become, and the person you wish to become. Loving yourself is fundamental in becoming secure and jealousy free, it is a skill that everyone should undertake, study and master, however it is a skill that many fail to achieve.

Dr. Maxwell Maltz author of the bestseller *Psycho-Cybernetics* wrote, "The goal of any psychotherapy is to change an individual's image of himself."

Your self-image is the image that you project to the world. The most important relationship you will ever have in your brief life upon this planet, is the one you will have with yourself, first and foremost. The relationship you have with your partner, family, friends or even your work colleagues are all but a reflection upon the way that you see and feel about yourself.

Love Is A State Of Mind

"Happiness is a choice – not a result. Nothing will make you happy until you choose to be happy. No person will make you happy unless you decide to be happy. Your happiness will not come to you. It can only come from you."
Ralph Marston.

People who are jealous are jealous because they are insecure and have low self-esteem. Therefore, to be free from jealousy you have to become as secure and happy as possible, and that means being able to love yourself. What is love? Where does love come from? Love, like happiness is a state of mind, LOVE is a DECISION. No one can give you love and happiness. You may well say, *"My partner makes me so happy."* Or *"I feel loved when I'm with my partner."* However, in truth, all of your emotions and feelings come from the inside out, not from the outside in. Feeling loved is all down to the way that you choose to see yourself and how you choose to see the world around you.

Susan says, *"Dave makes me feel so loved, without him in my life, life wouldn't be worth living."*

If only Susan could grasp the concept that the feeling of love that makes her feel so happy, already resides within herself, albeit undiscovered.

Imagine you're at a restaurant with your partner and you spill wine down your new top. How you react to this incident, is dependent upon how you choose to think about it. You could either: cry and stick your head in the pudding, or you could laugh it off so that you can enjoy the rest of your evening. **You have a choice in how you feel**. Charles R. Swindoll author of *The Grace Awakening*, *"Life is 10% what happens to you. And 90% how you react to it."* Charles was right. People who are happy in life, are not happy because everything always goes right for them. People who are happy in life have just the same sort of problems as people who are unhappy, the only difference is that happy people don't allow things that are out of their control to drag them down.

When you choose to give other people, such as your partner, responsibility for the love that you feel and the happiness that you have, you then give away control of your feelings, and your happiness then depends upon that person and their ability to be nice and loving towards you. And what happens if that person isn't nice to you, and they turn around and tell you that they don't love you anymore? The chances are, you would be devastated. You would feel as if your world has come to an end.

Love and happiness are a state of mind, you have to create from within. Once you have found your inner love and happiness, then no one can take it away from you.

Ten Things

"Be happy for this moment. This moment is your life."

Omar Khayyam.

A great way to find your self-love, is to begin by appreciating your good points. The things that make you special and unique. **Write a list of ten qualities about yourself that you feel are positive.** Are you a good listener? Are you hard working? Have you got a great sense of humour? It could be any attribute that you see about yourself as being positive.

If you find yourself struggling to write a list of just ten things that you find positive about yourself, don't worry most people who suffer with jealousy have a poor self-image and will find this exercise difficult. However, to free yourself from jealousy you must learn how to recognise and appreciate the things that make you special.

Fred's List:

1. I'm trustworthy.

2. I'm honest.

3. I'm always tidy.

4. I'm sensitive.

5. I always think of others.

6. I'm affectionate.

7. I'm loving.

8. I'm punctual.

9. I've got a good sense of humour.

10. I'm adventurous.

Once you have written down your list of ten positive attributes, pin it up somewhere where you can easily see it every day, perhaps on your fridge, or your bathroom mirror. Look at your list often and let your positive attributes sink into your unconscious mind. As soon as your unconscious mind begins to accept this new image of yourself, your self-image will change and over time you will start to feel special and unique, and eventually it will change who you are as a person. The object of this exercise is for your mind to get familiar and comfortable with your new positive self-image, so that you can begin to love yourself. **Whatever you look for in life, you will find. And whatever you think about you will become.**

Do Things You Love

"Happiness is not something you postpone for the future; it is something you design for the present."
Jim Rohn.

When was the last time you had fun? Many people feel guilty about doing something for themselves, when in fact it's just what most people need to do. We should all take a little time for yourself every now and then. **When you do the things that you love to do, it makes you feel good.** This in turn makes you feel more secure and leads to an increase in happy thoughts. If you think happy thoughts and feel good, you will also think and feel better towards other people, especially the people you love. Whatever it is that makes you happy, make the most of it. You are the most important person in your life, and all your other relationships will stem from how you treat yourself.

What do you love to do?

Things that Susan loves to do:

- I love watching old movies

- I love to travel

- I love to shop

- I love to go swimming

- I love to read a good thriller

- I love cats

What makes you happy? Once a week make it your priority to do the things that you love to do. Make a promise to yourself today to set a day in your diary to do something that you love: read the book you want to read, watch the movie you never got around to watching, book the flights to your dream destination. **Whatever it is, just do it!**

By doing the things you love, you will begin to see that YOU can take CONTROL of how you FEEL. You will also begin to notice that you feel more secure and positive and as your self-image becomes more positive, you will become less jealous. When you're in your happy place, your brain releases all those positive chemicals to make you feel good within yourself. This will impact how you feel about other people, especially your partner. **It's impossible to make your partner feel good if you don't feel good yourself. Love comes from within, not from without.**

Love Yourself First

1. Self-love is essential in becoming jealousy free.

2. If you don't love yourself, then how can you believe that someone else could love you?

3. The relationship you have with your partner, is but a reflection upon the way that you see and feel about yourself.

4. Love and happiness are a state of mind, you have to create from within.

Stop Comparing

"Comparison is the thief of joy."
Theodore Roosevelt.

D o you wish you were taller, slimmer, smarter or richer than you are? Most people would say yes. However, the feeling of inadequacy is prevalent in people who are jealous. **People who suffer with jealousy are constantly comparing themselves and their life to other people.** If you say, *"I wish I was slimmer"* ask yourself the question slimmer than who? Your neighbour? Your boss? Your best friend?

The problem with comparing yourself to other people, is that there will always be someone who is taller, slimmer, smarter and richer than you can ever be. To become secure and jealousy free, you have to learn how to love yourself for who you are now and appreciate the things you have in your life at this present moment. The writer Dale Carnegie once said, *"Success is getting what you want. Happiness is wanting what you get."*

Fred says, *"If I only looked like Tom Cruise. I would never be jealous because I know that Jane would never leave me."*

Fred probably isn't aware of the fact that Tom Cruise has been divorced numerous times. On the outside, other people and their lives appear more appealing than our own. Yet most people wish they could change one thing or another about themselves, even people such as Tom Cruise have their own challenges and concerns. Perhaps Tom Cruise wishes that he was a little taller, who knows!

Susan says, *"If only my boobs were bigger, I know it would stop Dave looking at other women."*

Even if Susan had boobs the size of Dolly Parton, Dave would probably still look at other women. If you're going to change yourself, then do it for yourself and never for someone else. Use other people and their lives as an inspiration to change the things within your own life that you are unhappy about. If you want to lose weight, then start eating healthier and exercising more. If you want to become smarter, read more books or enrol on a course. If you want to have more money, then don't spend more money than you earn or find a new job that pays more.

If you're not happy about something in your life that's within your control, then change it, don't just complain about it and wish you were someone else. **Be that person you want to be and achieve that which you want to achieve.** If however, there is something about yourself that you are not happy with that isn't in your control to change, such as your height or the colour of your eyes, then it's time to learn to love and accept yourself for who you are.

In the 2001 block buster comedy *Shallow Hal,* the main character Hal played by Jack Black, is an extremely shallow individual who judges people by the way they look. Hal is at a loss as to why true love and happiness seem to elude him, until one day, Hal gets stuck in a lift with the self-help guru Tony Robbins. Whilst dwindling away the time, Hal confides in Tony about his relationship problems. Feeling sorry for Hal, Tony decides to help him out by putting him into a hypnotic trance. For the first time in his life, Hal begins to see people for who they truly are. Hal's world is turned upside down after he meets Rosemary, who to the outside world is clinically obese. However, to Hal who can only see people's internal character, Rosemary is a beautiful, slim, blonde and for the first time in Hal's life he finds the love and happiness that he had been searching for all his life.

To be free from jealousy, you need to change your internal world just like Hal was able to. **When we first meet people, we don't really get to see the full image of who that person is.** For instance, you may see someone driving an expensive sports car like a Ferrari and think, *"Why can't I be like them? They look so happy and successful."* However, you don't know what's happening in their life right now. Their business may be in liquidation and they may be about to lose their home. They may have a bad temper and fall out with everyone, including their own family. Who knows? They may not be. They may be a great person and work 60 hours a week to drive that car. It's impossible to compare yourself with someone else, simply because you're not like anyone else, and no one else is like you. You are unique. You are special. You are the one and only you. **When you stop comparing yourself with other people, you can start living for who you are.**

Stop Comparing

1. People who suffer with jealousy are constantly comparing themselves and their life to other people.

2. If you're not happy about something in your life that is within your control, then change it.

3. Be that person you want to be and achieve that which you want to achieve.

4. It's impossible to compare yourself with someone else, simply because you're not like anyone else, and no one else is like you.

Don't Believe Everything You Think!

"Reality is merely an illusion, albeit a very persistent one."

Albert Einstein.

Our beliefs are what define us, they make us who we are. Our beliefs create our reality, as our reality is based on what we believe. **Whenever you believe in something your unconscious mind will accept that belief as a fact.** If you believe that one day your partner will leave you, your unconscious mind will automatically accept that belief as a fact and start looking for evidence to corroborate that fact. If you believe that your partner is still in love with their ex-partner, your unconscious mind will look for evidence to back that belief up and prove it as a fact. When you were a child, did you ever look up at the starry sky on Christmas Eve, hoping to catch a glimpse of the elusive Father Christmas? Or did you once believe that there lived a monster who lived under your bed, whose whole existence was to gobble you up

111

as soon as the lights were out? Whenever we believe something our mind turns that belief into reality.

Our mind plays tricks on us all the time. Have you ever lost your keys just before you had to go out? You search your pockets, check the floor, look down the sides of the chairs, you even check the door just in case you have left them in the keyhole. The keys seem to have dematerialised. The clock is ticking. You're starting to get stressed. You sit down to catch your breath and as if by magic, they appear right there in front of you on the table. The keys have been on the table, in plain sight, all this time. How could I have missed them you wonder! This is what's known as, a negative hallucination. Hallucinations are not just the result of taking a mind-altering psychotic drug such as LSD or marijuana, and they're not limited to people who suffer with mental health problems such as schizophrenia or bipolar disorder.

Close your eyes and think of the last time you had a beach holiday. What do you see in your mind's eye? Do you see people enjoying the sun? Do you see crystal clear water? Do you hear the sound of children playing? Can you feel the heat of the sun rays beating down upon your skin? Can you feel the grains of sand beneath your feet? Now open your eyes. To vividly relive such a pleasant memory, you must invoke your imagination. You consciously created a hallucination to produce the images that you saw and the sounds that you heard. This is what's known as a positive hallucination. **Hallucinations are a natural phenomenon. In fact, we hallucinate every day.**

You Are What You Believe You Are

"Think before you act on what you believe."
Bo Bennett.

Your beliefs can either help you to be happy and secure or unhappy and insecure. It's your beliefs that fundamentally make you, who you are. Your beliefs affect your relationships with your boss, your family, your partner and most importantly your relationship with yourself. In fact, everyone you will ever encounter throughout your entire life, will be affected by what you choose to believe.

When we are suffering with jealousy, our mind has a strange habit of making us believe the worst possible scenarios imaginable. Take poor Fred's for instance.

Fred says, *"If Jane did leave me, my life would come to an end. I can't help thinking the way I do."*

What would happen if Jane did leave Fred? Fred would feel like his life has come to an end because that's what Fred believes would happen. Fred lives in constant torment because of his beliefs. Fred believes that one day, his partner will either run away with one of her work colleagues or she will get back together with her ex-partner. However, Fred's biggest problem is that he believes that he can't help thinking the way he does. No wonder Fred feels so insecure and jealous.

How many times have you heard that old saying, *"I can't help the way I think"* yet what we choose to think about is in fact the only thing that we do have control over.

Susan says, *"What drives me nuts, is when I catch Dave looking at other women."*

If Susan believes that her partner shouldn't look at other women, Susan is going to be NUTS all the time. **In life you get what you believe, good or bad.**

Where Do Negative Beliefs Come From?

Most of our core beliefs are formed because of a strong emotional event within our life. Let's look at Fred for example: Fred was born in Ireland, his father died when he was a child leaving Fred to be raised by his mother. Fred was the eldest out of three children. Fred's mother was a stern, God fearing woman, who was never to be disobeyed. She had the temperament of 'Dr Jekyll and Mr Hyde,' one moment she could be kind and gentle, the next moment she could be cruel and ruthless. Fred was constantly berated by his oppressive mother.

Fred's mother says, *"Fred why are you so stupid? You are just like your useless father; God rest his soul. Always*

pretending to be nice, like the world is such a great place.
Well, I've got news for you my lad, the world is not a great
place, in fact it's a bad place and life will always be hard.
You mark my words my lad, you will never amount to
anything, just like your useless father. Now go and clean
your room before I show you the back of my hand."

One could say that Fred didn't have the best upbringing and one could conjecture that these early incidents in Fred's life could be the reason why he suffers with his negative beliefs. However, our beliefs don't always originate from our upbringing, they can also be developed later in life.

Let's take a look at Susan. When Susan was twenty-one, she had already been with Frank for over five years. They were engaged to be married and were very much in love. Susan believed that Frank was the man of her dreams, the man she would spend the rest of her life with, but it wasn't to be. One day, Frank phoned Susan at work and informed her that he had been unhappy for a long time and that he had in fact, met someone else. Susan was distraught, she felt like her world had ended. Susan later found out that "someone else," was in fact Frank's work colleague.

There are as many reasons for why people are insecure and jealous, as there are people. We have all got our own reasons for why we act the way we do. However, the good news is, to be secure and jealousy free, you don't need to know or even understand where your jealous beliefs originated from, to become free from them. All you need to know and understand is that you can choose what you want to believe and when you

115

change the way that you think, your beliefs and your behaviour will also change. **Negative beliefs are like gremlins that hide in your mind and cause havoc in your life.**

How To Change Your Beliefs

How do we change our jealous beliefs? The answer may be simpler than you first think. You just need to change the beliefs that make you feel insecure and jealous, to beliefs that make you feel happy and secure. Is it really that simple? The answer is YES. However, just because it's simple doesn't mean that it's easy. Most of your jealous beliefs will be deep rooted and hidden from your conscious awareness.

To change your negative beliefs, you must first be able to identify them. Begin by asking yourself the question, what makes me feel jealous? Write it down and make a list of everything that you can think of that that makes you feel jealous. Write the list as if you were talking to your partner. Under each reason, leave a space.

Fred's list of things that make him feel jealous:

• The clothes that you wear when you go out with your friends.

• When you talk to other men.

116

- When you are late home, I think it's because you're with someone else.
- When you are talking to your ex-partner.
- I think there is something going on between you and your boss.

Once you have completed the list of all the things that make you jealous, the next step is to see those things that make you feel jealous from a new perspective. Think of a new positive way you could view those things. You don't have to believe these new challenging statements to begin with, you just have to be able to come up with a new alternative way of seeing those negative beliefs. Write underneath each one, how you could see those things if you didn't suffer with jealousy.

Fred's alternative way of seeing those things:

- The clothes that you wear when you go out with your friends.
- **You wear clothes that make you feel good.**
- When you talk to other men.
- **There is nothing wrong in just talking.**

- When you are late, I think it's because you're with someone else.
- **I know that sometimes you have to work over and the traffic can be bad.**
- When you are talking to your ex-partner.
- **You may have loved your ex-partner but that's in the past and you're with me now. I know you love me very much.**
- I think there is something going on between you and your boss.
- **I know deep down that there's nothing going on with you and your boss and it's all in my head.**

Work your way through your list of things that make you feel jealous until you have challenged and changed them to a more positive way of seeing things. By doing this exercise you are allowing your unconscious mind to see things from a different perspective, opening up the possibilities of creating new positive beliefs.

Fred now says, *"I know that Jane talks to other men, but I also know that she loves me very much. And I trust her."*

Just by Fred simply changing the way that he CHOOSES to see things, Fred has also changed his belief about his partner talking to other men, in so doing, he has undoubtedly changed the way that he feels. Now Fred doesn't feel like he's going to blow a fuse every time Jane talks to another man.

You can't control the outside world. However, you can control the world that lies within you by controlling your thoughts and choosing what you want to dwell upon. **When you take control of your thoughts, you also take control of your feelings.** Your feelings are a reflection of your thoughts and what you are think about, is based on what you believe.

Once you start to think differently, you will start to feel differently and before you know it, you will start to develop new positive beliefs.

The reason this works, is because if you change how you think, you will change how you feel.

Don't Believe Everything You Think!

1. Your beliefs create your reality as your reality is based on what you believe.

2. Your mind plays tricks on you all the time.

3. Your beliefs can either help you to be happy and secure or unhappy and insecure.

4. When you change the way you choose to think, your beliefs and your behaviour will also change.

5. Once you start to think differently, you will start to feel differently.

Breaking The Trance

"One day, I went to buy something for my dad at the
shops, and I heard a song by Nat King Cole called
'Stardust Melody.' It was like I went into a trance or
something. I forgot all about my dad sending me to the
shop. When I got home, I explained to him what
happened. I thought I was going to get a whipping, but
he understood."
Desmond Dekker.

Near the beginning of this book we looked at how most of our behaviour, repeated often enough becomes automated, as if we were in some sort of trance like state. **To become jealousy free, we must learn how to break our automated trance like states so that we become conscious of our negative behaviour.** What is a trance state? When the word trance is mentioned most people would picture in their mind, the scene of a stage hypnotist making his subjects run around acting like chickens. Or the image of someone laying on a couch, with someone standing over them swinging a pocket watch side to side, inducing them into a hypnotic trance.

In the classic book, Guide To Trance Formation, Richard Bandler wrote, *"People are not simply in or out of trance but are moving from one trance to another."* **A trance state is a natural phenomenon.** You don't need a hypnotist to wave a watch under your nose or to put you under some sort of magical spell for you to be induced into a trance. A trance state is nothing more than being in an altered state of being. We put ourselves in and out of trance states every day. Whenever our attention is fixated on something in particular, we are in fact in a trance like state.

Have you ever been so engrossed in an activity such as reading a book or watching tv and suddenly you hear a sound which turns out to be someone calling your name? That someone, has in fact been calling your name for the last five minutes unbeknown to you. In times like these we generally use such phrases as, ***"Sorry I was miles away."*** Or ***"Sorry, I was away with the fairies."*** Yet we weren't miles away, and we weren't playing with the fairies. So why weren't we aware of our own name being called? Did our ears take a rest and shut up shop? The reason you weren't aware of someone calling your name was because you were in a trance and it wasn't until you started to shift your state of focus from the book or the TV screen that you were so engrossed in, that you became aware of someone calling your name.

Whenever we focus upon something, we automatically go into a trance like state and when we are in a trance like state our behaviour becomes automated.

Fred says, *"As soon as I hear Jane's ex-partner on the phone, I automatically become physically tense and my mind goes into a jealous fog."*

What Fred is describing is a classic sign of a trance like state. Fred doesn't need the apparatus of a swinging watch. Fred's trance like state is automatically triggered by the mere voice of Jane's ex-partner, which then triggers his automatic jealous behaviour.

To be free from jealousy your mind must become free from those triggers that automatically create your jealous behaviour. Therefore, to de-hypnotise yourself, it's essential for you to learn how to **identify** those **triggers.**

Feelings Follow Thoughts

Whenever we are suffering from a bout of jealousy, we are operating on autopilot brought on by a trance state. When we are in this jealous state our thoughts seem as though they are controlled by our uncontrollable feelings. This is the reason why people say things such as, *"I can't help feeling so jealous."* Or *"When I feel jealous, it's as though something just comes over me."* When in fact quite the opposite is true; **your feelings are the results of your thoughts that you choose to dwell upon.**

A great way to break your self-induced jealous state, is by changing what you dwell upon. Remember your feelings follow your thoughts, so whenever you choose to focus on something positive, you are inducing a new positive trance like state.

Fred changes his focus:

"Whenever I start to feel insecure and jealous, I close my eyes and imagine myself floating up above the world and into space. I then look down at the world and my life and see all the good things that I appreciate such as my family and friends. I then see myself floating back down into my body and open my eyes."

"Strangely enough, after a few seconds I don't feel so insecure and jealous. I just feel relaxed and calm."

Fred was able to break his automated jealous state by changing his focus which in turn changed the way that he felt. Fred was able to control his emotions, instead of his emotions controlling him.

The next time you start to feel insecure and jealous, change your focus and automatically you will change your feelings. You could perhaps imagine yourself relaxing on a hot tropical beach somewhere or even imagine yourself driving your dream car through the Alps. It doesn't really matter where you decide to take your mind, as long as it's somewhere that will make you feel good. **Wherever your mind goes, your feelings will follow.**

Thoughts Follow Action

"A competent and self-confident person is incapable of jealousy in anything. Jealousy is invariably a symptom of neurotic insecurity."

Robert A. Heinlein.

Our feelings not only follow our thoughts, but our thoughts also follow (action) what we do. Take for instance the last time you did something that you weren't that keen on doing; let's say the garage was full of junk and needed cleaning out, your MIND is saying, *"I'll do it next week"* or *"It's not that bad."* Begrudgingly you decide it must be sorted today. You start to pack things away, you throw out the junk and before you know it, you're beginning to feel good about cleaning it out and you wished you would had done it months ago.

If you find yourself struggling to break your jealous trance like state, you can use this technique of changing your thought pattern by changing what you are physically doing. Remember, **thoughts** follow **action,** just like our cleaning out the garage example. The next time you start to feel insecure and jealous, do something physical, anything as long as you're moving your body. Whenever you do a physical activity, your body will start to release endorphins that naturally begin to make you feel better. Once you start to feel better, your thoughts will also start to improve.

You could:

- Go to the gym

- Go for a walk

- Go swimming

- Do some chores that need doing

- Take your dog for a walk

- Do some sit ups

It doesn't matter what you do, as long as you do something.

Susan says, *"Whenever I start to feel insecure and jealous, I go out and take the dog for a walk. Just to change the way I'm thinking. And it works. Once I've been out with the dog, I feel better. I don't feel so stressed and insecure."*

By doing something physical you are breaking your focus, which will also break your jealous trance.

Breaking The Trance

1. A trance state is a natural phenomenon.

2. To become jealousy free, we must learn how to break our automated trance like states so that we become conscious of our behaviour.

3. When you choose to focus on something positive, you will feel positive.

4. Feelings not only follow our thoughts, but our thoughts also follow what we do.

5. The next time you start to feel insecure and jealous, do something physical. By doing something physical you are breaking your focus, which will also break your jealous trance.

Chapter 3

How To Help Your Partner To Be
Jealousy Free

Ready & Willing

Do I Make My Partner Jealous?

Jealous Beliefs, Jealous Behaviour

Your Partners Motive To Change

Ask Your Partner To Read This Book

Share Your Thoughts & Feelings

Taking Time Out!

When It's Time To End The Relationship

When You Change, Your Partner Has To Change

How To Help Your Partner To Be Jealousy Free

This section of the book is a guide for people who are in a relationship with someone who is suffering from jealousy and who want to help them to be jealousy free. The old adage, **"You can't help who you fall in love with,"** may well be true however, **we can choose who we want to be our life partner.**

Being in a relationship with someone who suffers from jealousy and who constantly wants to know of your whereabouts and who you have been talking to, is emotionally and physically draining. If you are in a new relationship the signs of jealousy can be so minor that you hardly notice them. Most people in a new relationship are on their best behaviour and try to show only their best attributes. Even if we do get to see a character flaw near the beginning of the relationship, most people often decide to brush over such conduct thinking naively that such behaviour can be ironed out in the future.

Helping your partner to change their insecure jealous ways will not be a quick and easy task, it will take time and

effort; **how much time and effort will depend upon how ready and willing your partner is to make the changes that are necessary for them to become jealousy free.** It's important to be aware of the fact that you cannot change your partner, as long-lasting change has to come from within.

You say, *"If I can't change my partner, then what can I do?"*

Your role will be to support your partner to help them change themselves by using the techniques within this book. **Using the techniques within this book can help you, to help your partner on their journey to be jealousy free.** If your partner isn't ready and willing to change, then sadly there isn't much that you can accomplish by trying to help them. One of the greatest pitfalls that must be avoided when trying to help someone who suffers with jealousy, is trying to help that person when they are neither willing nor ready to change.

The next section of this book will help you to identify if your partner is ready and willing to change. **At times it may seem daunting and perhaps a bit overwhelming trying to help someone change their jealous ways. Take heart though,** Lao Tzu once said, *"A journey of a thousand miles begins with a single step,"*

Ready & Willing

"Change your thoughts and you change your world."

Norman Vincent Peale.

How do you know if your partner is ready and willing to change? You may be lucky and have a partner who freely admits to having a problem with jealousy. *"I know I'm jealous. But I can't help the way I am."* If your partner admits to suffering with jealousy, see it as a positive sign because what they are fundamentally saying, albeit at an unconscious level is, *"I know I have a problem, but I don't know how to fix it."* Your partner's words will reveal their thoughts and feelings. This can give you vital insight into determining if your partner is ready and willing to become jealousy free.

More often than not, people who suffer from jealousy will be less revealing, in which case you will have to look out for subtle clues that may give you an inclination regarding your partner's position in wanting to change and their willingness to change.

Does your partner say any of the following?

- I'm sorry for the way I am.

- I can't help the way I am.

- I want to be different.

- I wish I was different.

- I know you love me, but I always think the worst.

- I wish things were different.

- I know it's me and not you.

- I'll try to change.

- I hate the way I am.

If your partner is using such statements as the above or very similar, then that's great news because all the above statements basically boil down to: *"I want to change, I just don't know how to change."* With such information, you will then know that your partner is ready and willing to change. Only when you're certain that your partner is ready and willing to change, can you begin the process of helping your partner to become jealousy free.

No Signs!

What if I don't see any indication that my partner is ready and willing to change their jealous ways? If you find that your partner isn't giving you any indication that they are ready and willing to change, don't be too concerned particularly if you are in a fairly new relationship, as most people at the beginning of a relationship tend to hide some of their feelings. If, however, over time your partner still shows you no indication that they are ready and willing to change their jealous ways, then you have no choice but to be decisive and open with your partner about how you really feel.

Jane says, *"I can't stand the constant questions, "Where have you been?" "Who have you been talking to?" I feel like a prisoner. I can't take it anymore. I don't think it's working."*

Fred says, *"Please don't leave me, I'm beginning you. I promise I'll change. Give me a chance."*

For some people who suffer from jealousy, it may well take a critical moment of truth before they can begin to open up about their thoughts and feelings regarding their jealousy. Generally, people who do suffer from jealousy do want to change their negative, insecure ways, it's just that they either don't know how or they wrongly believe that they can't change.

Not Ready & Willing

How will I know if my partner isn't ready or willing to change their jealous ways? You will know through your partner's words. Your partner's words will reveal your partner's thoughts and feelings about changing their jealous ways.

Dave says, *"I feel suffocated. I love you, but I can't go on like this any longer."*

Susan says, *"Suit yourself. I'm not changing. You're the one with the problem."*

If your partner isn't ready and willing to change then it's time to skip straight to the chapter, **Take Time Out** near the end of this book.

Does your partner say any of the following?

- I'm not the one with the problem!

- You are the one with problem!

- I won't change for anyone!

- You are the one that needs to change!

- I'm ok with the way I am!

- I wish you were different!

- I'm happy with how things are!

- I'm not jealous!

Having a partner who shows no inclination of being ready or willing to change their jealous ways, may need the radical steps that are outlined in **Take Time Out** for them to want to change.

Ready & Willing

1. If your partner admits to suffering with jealousy, see it as a positive.

2. Only when you're certain that your partner is ready and willing to change, can you begin the process of helping your partner to become jealousy free.

3. Generally, people who do suffer from jealousy do want to change their negative, insecure ways. They either don't know how or they wrongly believe that they can't change.

4. If your partner isn't ready and willing to change, then sadly there isn't much that you can accomplish in helping them.

Do I Make My Partner Jealous?

Do I make my partner jealous? The short answer is NO! It's impossible for you to make anyone else feel jealous, including your partner. **Jealousy is just like any other feeling; it is subjective not objective.** Your partner's emotions and feelings come from the inside out, not from the outside in. It has nothing to do with how you dress, who you talk to or who your friends are. It's your partner who makes themselves jealous with their insecure feelings and jealous thoughts.

Sadly, most people who do suffer with jealousy themselves, believe that their jealous feelings are somehow caused objectively through other people's (mainly their partner's) perceived inappropriate behaviour. However, problems occur when the person held responsible for causing their jealousy, starts to believe it themselves.

Does your partner say any of the following?

- You make me jealous.

- I can't trust you.

- I wasn't jealous until I met you.

- You make me feel this way.

The Rabbit Hole

Jane says, *"I sometimes think that the reason why Fred is jealous is because of me. Maybe I am too friendly, maybe I do give off the wrong impressions to other men."*

Have you started to believe that perhaps you are the reason for your partner's jealousy? Have you found yourself questioning your own behaviour? It's far too easy to get sucked down the rabbit hole of paranoia and insecurity. The danger is when you start to believe it yourself. If you allow your partner's (false) belief to become your belief, then you will never be in a position to help your partner to become jealousy free.

You must remain resolute within your own mind knowing that the reason why your partner suffers with jealousy is NOT because of YOU. You don't make your partner feel jealous; jealousy comes from within not from without. Jealousy, like happiness is a state of mind. Your partner makes themselves jealous. **The reason why your partner suffers with jealousy is because of the way they think.**

Do I Make My Partner Jealous?

1. It's impossible for you to make anyone else feel jealous.

2. Jealousy is subjective not objective.

3. Most people who suffer with jealousy themselves, believe that their jealousy is caused objectively through other people's perceived inappropriate behaviour.

4. The reason why you partner suffers with jealousy is because of the way they think.

Jealous Beliefs, Jealous Behaviour

"Only I can change my life.
No one can do it for me."
Carol Burnett.

It is our core beliefs that will either give us the relationship of our dreams or the relationship of our nightmares. Negative beliefs will smother and destroy a relationship before it has a chance to grow and flourish. Negative beliefs are the enemy of happiness and security. **Fundamentally, jealous beliefs lead to jealous behaviour.**

For you to be successful in helping your partner to be free from the shackles of jealousy, it is fundamental for you to become aware of your partner's negative beliefs, as it's these beliefs that are the cause of their insecure ways. **Jealousy cannot exist without negative beliefs.** The task of finding out the underlying beliefs that are the cause of your partner's jealousy may not be an easy undertaking, particularly if your partner's negative beliefs are at an unconscious level.

Some negative beliefs that can lead to jealousy:

- People are dishonest.

- People are untrustworthy.

- Life will always go wrong.

- Happiness is unachievable.

Lead By Example

So how do you go about the task of uncovering your partners negative beliefs? A great way to help your partner be more open about their beliefs is for you to lead by example. **If you believe your partner doesn't trust you, then share that thought with your partner. If you think that your partner still believes that you're trying to get back with your ex-partner, then share those thoughts and feelings.** The objective of this sharing exercise is for you to open up an avenue of truth between you, so that you can lead your partner into sharing some of their negative beliefs that may be the root cause of their jealousy.

Leading by example:

Dave says, *"Susan, I love you very much. But I think that you are not happy with who I am."*

Susan says, *"What are you talking about?"*

Dave says, *"I feel like I'm walking on eggshells whenever I'm around you. I feel like I can't be my true self anymore. I have reservations about what I should, and shouldn't say to you, just in case you take things the wrong way. Barry from work asked me if I wanted to go out last weekend, I said no, I didn't say anything to you about it because I know it would have caused a problem. You over analyse everything I say and do. Things have to change."*

Susan says, *"I'm sorry Dave, I love you very much. I can't ever imagine being without you. I just think that I'm not good enough for you and that one day you will meet someone better than me, someone younger and better looking and then you will be gone for good, and I will be left heartbroken."*

In this example, by Dave sharing some of his own thoughts and feelings, he was able to get to the bottom of his partner's negative belief system that was causing Susan to feel so jealous. He found out that his partner believed that she wasn't good enough or worthy enough of love. He also found out that his partner believed that he was going to leave her one day for someone younger and better looking. With this new insight, Dave was then able to address the negative beliefs by explaining what he truly thought and felt about his partner.

Dave says, *"Susan, if I wasn't happy with you then I wouldn't be with you. I'm with you because I love you. You are beautiful. I don't want to be with anyone else, I would never cheat on you. If anytime in the future, I did feel that I didn't want to be with you I would tell you."*

By admitting to your partner some of your own core self-beliefs you can then give your partner the encouragement and incentive that they may need in order to share some of their own beliefs. **Remember though, your partner's negative beliefs that cause their jealousy, can be so deeply rooted within their unconscious mind, they may not even know that these are causing them any issues.**

Ask The Question

If you find that you're struggling to discover what your partner's negative beliefs are, you can try the direct route and simply ask your partner. If for example, your partner always asks who you have spoken to, then ask them why they want to know? If your partner makes a scene whenever you are running late, then ask why? Be direct and demand an answer. When your partner understands you're serious, your partner will have to give a serious answer.

Ask the question:

Jane says, *"Fred why is it whenever I'm late from work, you always ask me loads of questions. Why do you always question my whereabouts and actions?"*

Fred says, *"I don't always question you."*

Jane says, *"Fred you do, and it makes me feel uncomfortable, so I want to know why. What's going on?"*

Fred says, *"Ok if you really want to know the truth. When you're late from work, for some stupid reason, I've got it in my head that you're with your ex-partner and for some mad reason I still think that you love him."*

With just a few simple but direct questions, Jane was able to identify some of her partner's negative beliefs that cause him to be so insecure and jealous.

Challenge your partner's jealous behaviour, see if you can discover an insight into what it is that causes them to be so jealous. Keep in mind though, what you are trying to do is obtain what deep seated beliefs your partner holds onto to causing them to feel so jealous. Expect to come up against resistance and remember, don't take it personally. If your partner is similar to Fred, where their negative beliefs are practically spilling out and it's almost impossible to control their thoughts and feelings, then your task of identifying those negative beliefs will be far easier. It will be through your partner's thoughts and behaviour that it becomes possible to discover their underlying beliefs that cause their jealousy.

Once Identified

Once you have become aware of your partners negative beliefs that cause them to be jealous, you're then able to help them become jealousy free by addressing and correcting their false beliefs. For example, Jane discovered that one of her partner's negative beliefs that made him feel so jealous was that he believed that she was having a secret liaison with her ex-partner whom he believed she still had romantic feelings for. Whenever she's running late, it automatically triggers her partner to feel jealous. Jane, now armed with such valuable insights, can now begin to alleviate her partner's negative beliefs by dealing with any future circumstances in which she's going to be running late, by simply giving her partner a quick call or text to inform him of the situation.

Jane phones Fred, *"Hi sweetie, I just wanted to let you know that the work conference is running over so I'm going to be running late, hopefully not too long. I will call you when I'm on my way home. I love you."*

Fear cannot live, where knowledge resides. The old adage, **knowledge is power** is so true. What are your partner's negative beliefs that cause them to be jealous? Once you discover what they are, you will be in a great position of knowledge to be able to help quash and alleviate some of those false negative beliefs.

Jealous Beliefs, Jealous Behaviour

1. Jealous beliefs lead to jealous behaviour.

2. Become aware of your partner's jealous beliefs.

3. By admitting to your partner some of your own core self-beliefs, you can then give your partner the encouragement and incentive they may need in order to share some of their own beliefs.

4. It will be through your partner's thoughts and behaviour that it becomes possible to discover their underlying beliefs that cause their jealousy.

Your Partner's Motive To Change

"Being deeply loved by someone gives you strength, while loving someone deeply gives you courage."

Lao Tzu.

Your partner, like most people in life will not want to change, it's a fact of life that people don't like to change because it makes them feel uncomfortable. People love the comfort of routine, whether that routine is good for them or not. **To be able to help your partner change their jealous ways, your partner has to have a good enough reason to change** and what better motive can your partner have, than for the person they love. You have to become that reason for change. **The love that you have for your partner, will be your partner's motivation to think, feel and behave differently.** However, the truth of the matter is, unless your partner feels and more importantly believes, that they are loved by you, your partner will not have the motivation to make the changes that are necessary to be jealousy free.

On The Same Page!

By the mere fact that you are reading this book it's obvious that you love your partner. To be able to help your partner become jealousy free, your partner has to know and feel that they are loved by you. **The trouble with love is that love, like any other feeling is subjective, not objective.** We all receive and give love in our own way based upon our character. Just because you express love to your partner in your own personal way doesn't necessarily mean that your partner feels loved. For instance, you may be the type of person who expresses love verbally and therefore, you may tell your partner how much you love them every day. Consequently, you believe that your partner knows that they are loved when in fact, your partner may respond only to the physical expression of love, such as being intimate, hugging, kissing or just holding hands.

Jane says, *"Fred knows how much I love him, I tell him every day."*

Fred says, *"I know Jane tells me that she loves me all the time, but I just don't feel it, I wish she was a bit more affectionate."*

You may be a physical type of person and therefore, it comes naturally to you to express your love by being physical with your partner when in fact, your partner may be someone who needs to be told how much you love them and how much they mean to you to feel loved.

Dave says, *"Susan knows that I love her. I'm always holding her hand whenever we are out, I kiss her every day, I'm really affectionate."*

Susan says, *"Dave can be a bit overbearing sometimes. He always wants to be close to me, I know it's his way of showing me that he loves me but sometimes I just wish that we could sit down and talk about how we really feel about each other."*

Speaking The Same Language

Why is it that some people only feel love when it's physically expressed to them, whilst other people feel love when it's being verbalised to them? The reason is because we are all different, we all experience love in our own unique way. A group of people go to the cinema and they all watch the same movie, some people find the movie boring and fall asleep, some people find the movie funny, and some people find the movie so dreadful they get up and walk out.

How can the same movie have such a varied effect on people? After all, everyone in the cinema watches the same movie and hears the same lines. The reason is that we all perceive things differently, although generally we often share the same likes and dislikes. For instance, it would be a fair statement to say that most people like chocolate however, some people don't. Most people don't like spiders, yet there are some people who love spiders. We all think and feel differently, it's what distinguishes each and every one of us. **When it comes to our partner's likes and dislikes, we can often presume that they are the same as our own. But this isn't always the case, and how you receive love can be the opposite to how your partner does.**

Kinaesthetic Or Auditory

What is it exactly that makes your partner feel loved? To be able to help your partner to be free from jealousy, it's paramount for you to know the answer to this question. If you are unsure what it is that makes your partner feel loved, then you will have to look into what it is that makes your partner feel special. How does your partner respond when you tell them how much you love them and how much they mean to you? Do they respond positively or are they dismissive of what you say? How does your partner respond when you physically express how much you love them? Do they respond positively to your tangible expression of love or are they dismissive of physical contact?

You will generally find that your partner will either be a kinaesthetic, physical receiver of love, which means it's more what you do, than what you say that counts. Or your partner will be an auditory type of person, someone who loves to talk and prefers to be told how much you love them and why they are so special to you.

People who are a kinaesthetic type of person feel loved when it is expressed visibly and through the medium of physical contact.

Kinaesthetic partners love:

- Feeling loved

- Being touched

- Being physically close to their partner

- Being kissed

- Having cuddles

- Being intimate

People who are an auditory type of person feel loved when love is expressed through the medium of words.

Auditory partners love:

- Being told that they are loved

- Deep and intimate conversations

- Being listened to

- Receiving compliments

- Talking about the future

- Receiving love notes/letters.

Whatever it is that makes your partner feel loved you must know what it is in order to have any chance of being able to help them free themselves from jealousy. Remember, you are your partner's motive to change. **Once you know what it is that makes your partner feel loved, all you need to do, is more of it.** If for instance, you find that your partner is more of a kinaesthetic sort of person, then begin to express your emotions of love in a more physical way. If on the other hand you find that your partner is more of an auditory type of person and likes to be told how much you love them and why they are so special to you, then simply by doing more of that your partner will be more open and receptive to change. **Your love for your partner will be like rocket fuel that will motivate them in becoming jealousy free.**

Dave says, *"I've started to listen to Susan more and share what I've been thinking and feeling about our future together."*

Susan says, *"Dave has changed so much, we talk all the time now. I feel that we have become so much closer. I know he loves me, and I love him so much."*

Jane says, *"Since I've started to show my love in a more physical way, Fred seems to be so much happier and he doesn't seem so stressed anymore."*

Fred says, *"Jane is totally different now, she's far more loving. I feel differently too; I really feel loved. Plus, I don't get as anxious as I used to."*

You have to find what works for your partner and do it more often. You must be their inspiration to change and become a better person. The ability in knowing what makes your partner feel loved, is probably the most important step you can take towards helping your partner become free from jealousy.

Your Partner's Motive To Change

1. People don't like to change because it makes them feel uncomfortable.

2. Your partner has to have a good enough reason to change.

3. You must become that reason for change.

4. What is it exactly that makes your partner feel loved?

5. Is your partner a kinaesthetic type of person or is your partner an auditory type of person?

6. Your love for your partner will be the rocket fuel that will motivate them to become jealousy free.

157

Ask Your Partner To Read This Book!

"No one knows if a book is good until they read the book."

Victor La Valle.

If you want your partner to be jealousy free, then why not just ask them to read this book or even to just read the section on **How To Be Jealousy Free**.

We are after all living in the 21st century, a time where all the information that has already been given to the world is only a click away for anyone who wants to educate themselves. Whether that information is for setting up a new business venture, learning a new language or for reading a self-help book like this one. The times that we now find ourselves in allow us to be able to read a whole book on our smart phone.

This book was written not only to help people like yourself, who want to help their partner to become jealousy free, it was also written to help people who suffer with jealousy. By reading and implementing the techniques within this book, you can learn to change your own negative ways.

Dave says, *"I've bought this book, I thought you may want to have a look."*

Susan says, *"What's it about?"*

Dave says, *"It's a self-help book on how to become jealousy free."*

Susan says, *"Ok, I'll take a look, perhaps it can help, it certainly won't do me any harm."*

If your partner is like Susan, who is ready and willing to take a look at this book, your role in helping them to become jealousy free will be far easier than trying to do it on your own. However, you may have a partner who is negative and thinks that reading such a book wouldn't be of any use. If your partner rejects the idea of reading this book, don't give up! Just leave the book somewhere where your partner can easily find it. Maybe by the side of the bed or under the coffee table, somewhere not too conspicuous, don't be tempted to put the book under their pillow, or in their lunch box, as the book will probably end up in the recycling bin. If your partner really is serious about wanting to change and make the relationship work, then they will take a look.

Thankfully, there are more people like Susan in the world today, who are able and willing to see the benefits of reading a book on self-help. Taking responsibility for our own behaviour is continually becoming more and more popular each year. The beauty of this book is that your partner doesn't have to read all of the book, for them to benefit from it. Imagine what can be achieved if your partner reads this book as well as yourself, double the results, bonus!

If you don't ask, the answer will always be no!

Ask Your Partner To Read This Book

1. This book was written not only to help people like yourself, who want to help their partner become jealousy free, it was also written for people who suffer with jealousy, to help them change their own negative ways.

2. If your partner is really serious about wanting to change and to make the relationship work, then they will take a look.

Share Your Thoughts & Feelings

"Honesty is the first chapter in the book of wisdom."
Thomas Jefferson.

If you feel like you are at your wits end and feel like jumping on a plane to the other side of the world because your partner's jealous behaviour is driving you nuts, then it's time to share your thoughts and feelings with your partner. To be able to help your partner to be jealousy free, you have to set the benchmark. You must set an example for your partner to follow. Be open with your partner and share your thoughts and feelings. **Keeping your thoughts and feelings bottled up doesn't work.** Sooner or later, your partner will figure out that something isn't right and because of their jealousy they will more than likely assume the worst possible reason for your unfamiliar and unusual behaviour.

Bottled up thoughts & feelings:

Fred says, *"What's wrong with you?"*

Jane says, *"What do you mean, what's wrong with me?"*

Fred says, *"You know what I mean. Every time I ask what you've been up to today, you go all quiet and coy on me. What's wrong?"*

Jane says, *"No I don't. You're being paranoid again. Why do you always have to start trouble?"*

Fred says, *"I'm not starting trouble. The way you react makes me think that you're trying to hide something from me, and I just want to know what it is. Have you met someone else? I just want to know the truth."*

Jane says, *"No I haven't met someone else, but think what you like. You always presume the worst anyway. You always make me feel like I'm doing something wrong and if you want to know the real truth Fred, I'm sick and tired of your jealous ways and I'm sick and tired of this relationship."*

Although Fred wasn't aware of the reasons behind his partner's unusual behaviour, Fred knew that something wasn't quite right. Fred, being insecure and jealous instinctively presumed the worst and because Jane had bottled up her thoughts and feelings for so long, they eventually came spilling out in the wrong way.

Trying to bury your thoughts and feelings does not work; eventually your thoughts and feelings will come spilling out, usually at the wrong time, in the wrong place. Strong thoughts and feelings are impossible to keep hidden; they eventually begin to show on the outside. The stronger the thoughts and feelings are that are being repressed, the stronger the inconsistencies will be in the behaviour. **Your behaviour will always betray your hidden thoughts and feelings.**

It's impossible not to communicate; did you know that the human face alone is made up of forty-three muscles? This is why sometimes we can look at someone's face and (instinctively) know what that person is thinking and feeling, without them saying a word. Some experts say that 90% of communication is nonverbal and HOW we say things, can be more important than WHAT we say. Take the word 'no' for instance, the word 'no' can be expressed in many ways with many different intentions behind the word. For instance, *"I said NO!"* can communicate our annoyance at someone. The word 'no' can also be expressed in a jovial, tongue in cheek way to express our happiness and surprise, *"No! You didn't..."* As a child, we knew within a matter of seconds if one of our parents was in a bad mood just by the tone of their voice, *"Dad!"* ... *"WHAT?"* ... *"Nothing, it doesn't matter. I'll ask Mom."* Our tone of voice, behind the words we use to communicate, is just as important as the words themselves.

Trust Is Based On Truth

To be able to help your partner to be jealousy free you must be prepared to share your thoughts and feelings. You need to be honest with your partner, don't try to keep your thoughts and feelings inside. You may think it would be easier not to cause a fuss, when in truth by withholding your true thoughts and feelings you are becoming part of the problem, instead of being part of the solution. After all, **if we can't be honest with the person whom we are supposed to love, then who can we be honest with?**

Truth & Honesty:

Jane says, *"Fred I love you and I want us to work, but I feel exhausted with your jealous ways. The constant, "where are you going?" "What time will you be back?" "Who have you been talking to?" It's all too much. I'm sorry, I don't know how much more I can take."*

Fred says, *"I'm so sorry. Please don't leave me. I don't want to lose you. I know I have a problem. I promise I will change. Give me a chance to be different. I will be different, I promise. I don't know what I would do without you in my life. I love you."*

Don't try to keep your thoughts and feelings inside, be honest with your partner about what you are thinking and feeling. After all, how can you expect your partner to be open and truthful with their thoughts and feelings if you don't do so yourself! Have the courage to speak your mind and communicate how you think and feel.

When you get better at being honest with your own thoughts and feelings, your partner will follow. **The only way your relationship can move forward is by being honest, not only with your partner, but with yourself also.**

Share Your Thoughts & Feelings

1. Strong thoughts and feelings are impossible to keep hidden; they eventually begin to show on the outside.

2. Your behaviour will betray your hidden thoughts and feelings.

3. Be open with your partner and share your thoughts and what you are feeling.

4. Have the courage to speak your mind and communicate how you think and feel.

Taking Time Out

"It's very important that we re-learn the art of resting and relaxing. Not only does it help prevent the onset of many illnesses that develop through chronic tension and worrying; it allows us to clear our minds, focus, and find creative solutions to problems."

Thich Nhat Hanh.

Taking time out is essentially taking a step back from the relationship without ending the relationship. Having a break from your partner can ultimately be the last hope in saving the relationship. **Countless relationships that have been ruined because of jealousy could have been saved by simply taking time out.** When you take time out from a relationship, you not only give yourself the space and time that you may need in establishing whether you want to continue the relationship without the undue pressure, it also gives your partner that time and space to contemplate the seriousness of the situation.

If you are at the stage where you are considering taking time apart, then it's time to inform your partner what you are contemplating, don't just spring the idea on them, give your partner fair warning that you are considering such action unless their behaviour changes for the better. **Taking time out can be a great wake up call for both of you.**

When should you take time out?

- When you are not sure about your feelings towards your partner.

- When you don't know how your partner feels towards you.

- When you feel that you have reached your breaking point.

- When you realise you can't think straight.

- When your partner isn't willing or ready to change.

When you feel you have reached that stage in the relationship where you feel like you can't take any more of your partner's jealous behaviour, then it's time to take time out. Once you have decided that it's time to take time out, stick with it. You then have to decide on what length of time you need to have apart. **How long should you take apart? As long as you think you need.** There is no magic number of days or weeks. The purpose of taking time out, is for you both to have the time and space needed to establish whether you want to continue the relationship. If you decide to have a week apart and you find your partner is being just as obstinate or you still haven't decided on what you want to do, then it's time to take another week or so, until you are confident in your decision or until your partner is ready and willing to change.

If you're not living together then taking time out will be far easier than if you were living together. If you do live together, the question is who should leave? The answer to that question depends on yours and your partner's circumstances. **It doesn't really matter who leaves as long as you both have that time and space to think things through. If your partner won't or can't leave for whatever reason, then you will have to take that first step.**

Be Prepared For Resistance

Don't expect your partner who is insecure and jealous to be over the moon with your decision to take time apart. **Your partner will more than likely think your decision is unnecessary and the wrong choice, so be prepared for resistance.** Here are three of the most common reactions to expect when you tell your partner you're taking a break.

Most common reactions:

1.   Don't leave me!

2. I don't care!

3. Have you found someone else?

1. Don't Leave Me!

If your partner's reaction to your decision to take a break from the relationship is, "Don't Leave Me" it's important to not get side-tracked and allow your partner to change your mind. You must be prepared to stick with your decision of taking time apart. **Don't get caught up and swayed by your partner's promises of sudden change.** You must stay firm and resolute in the knowledge that this decision is the best decision for you, and it may well be the last hope in saving your relationship in the long term. Inform your partner that you are intent on taking this time out and that you will be back on such a date.

Dave says, *"You've been saying for weeks now that things will change, and nothing has, in fact things seem to be getting worse between us. I can't take any more! I told you that unless your jealous behaviour changes then I think it would be best if we take some time apart. Well, nothing has changed, so I'm going to stay with Pete for a week."*

Susan says, *"I'm begging you; Dave please don't go. I can't cope on my own without you. Please, please, don't go."*

Dave says, *"I'm going tomorrow. Perhaps the time that we spend apart can help us in some way."*

When your partner knows that you are serious about your decision to take a break from the relationship, your partner will most likely feel totally distraught at the thought of not being together. This could mean they resort to practically anything, including begging to try and change your mind.

Here are a few examples of what your partner may say:

- I will change I promise!

- I can't live without you!

- I'm begging you don't go!

- Just give me one more chance!

2. I Don't Care!

If your partner responds with an "I Don't Care" kind of reaction your decision to take time out will be far easier to implement than if your partner responds with a "Don't Leave Me" or "Have You Found Someone Else?"

Jane says, *"Fred I love you and I want our relationship to work, but unless you're willing to at least try and make the changes that you've promised, then I want us to have a break. I'm going to stay at my mother's until..."*

Fred says, *"Do whatever you want. I don't care. It's not me with the problem, you're the one with the problem. Don't expect me to be waiting for you when you decide to come back. If we separate now then that's it, we are finished."*

Here are a few examples of what your partner may say:

- Do what you want!

- If you leave me now, then we are finished!

- I was right, I knew you would leave me!

- I was going to suggest we break up anyway!

Again, at this stage it's important not to be swayed by your partner's response. Stay strong and focused, remember that taking time out can ultimately be the last hope in saving your relationship.

3. Have You Found Someone Else?

Having a partner who responds with "Have You Found Someone Else?" will be the most difficult to deal with. For your partner believes that the only reason you want time apart is because there is someone else in your life.

Dave says, *"I can't put up with all of these constant accusations all of the time, I'm sick and tired. I'm moving out."*

Susan says, *"I knew it. Are you getting back with your ex-partner?"*

Here are a few examples of what your partner may say:

- I knew you would leave me for someone else!

- There's got to be someone else!

- I knew you were cheating!

- You're lying!

If your partner responds with similar comments to those above, you should be prepared for negative accusations to be thrown at you. However, it's important to remember to keep your cool and stay in control whilst your partner relinquishes their control. Don't allow yourself to get sucked into your partner's negative world. You don't have to justify your decision. **If your partner has it in their head that you're taking a break because there is someone else, then that is your partner's prerogative, it is not your responsibility to prove otherwise.**

Stick With Your Decision

No matter how your partner reacts to your decision to taking a break, it's important to stick with your decision. By the mere fact that you are reading this section of the book, you have more than likely already reached your breaking point. It's critical that you don't let your partner sway your thoughts regardless of what they say.

What happens if after a few days, your partner contacts you and begs you to come back home, what should you do? After all, your partner may only need one day to come to the conclusion that they have to change or risk losing you for good. What you must do is resist the temptation of giving into them, you must stay determined to see the process through to the end. By doing so, you are showing your partner how serious you are about them changing their jealous ways.

Having the time apart will help you establish your thoughts and feelings and will also give your partner the space and time needed to sort out their thoughts and feelings. **Sometimes in life when you want to keep something, you must be prepared to lose that very thing, in order to keep it.**

Taking Time Out

1. Taking time out is basically taking a step back from the relationship without ending the relationship.

2. Taking time out can be a great wake up call for both of you.

3. Inform your partner of what you are considering.

4. If you feel that you have reached a breaking point in the relationship, then it's time to take time out.

5. Stay strong and focused. Remember that taking time out can ultimately be the last hope in saving the relationship.

6. Stay determined to stay the course, to see the process through to the end.

When It's Time To End The Relationship

"When it's time for me to walk away from something, I walk away from it. My mind, my body, my conscience tells me that enough is enough."

Jerry West.

Being in a relationship with a partner who is insecure and jealous is by far one of the most frustrating and difficult predicaments to be in. Especially knowing full well that if it wasn't for their jealous behaviour you could potentially have a great future together. However, there may come a time when a relationship has run its course and becomes so toxic that we must accept the uncomfortable fact that the relationship must end. **Making the decision to end a relationship is one of the hardest decisions to be made.** However, self-preservation must be paramount, after all we are only on this Earth once, life is fragile, life is brief, we must make the most of our precious time whilst we are here.

If you have fallen out of love or if your partner is not ready or willing to change, then it's time to walk away. **If your partner won't allow you to help them up in life, then you mustn't allow them to pull you down.** Sometimes the only way we can help people in life, is by having the courage and the strength to let that person go and in doing so, give them the opportunity to find their own path in life. Although the decision to end a relationship is never an easy one to make, nowadays people are less likely to stay with a partner who they are unhappy with and don't love. Unlike only a few decades ago, where it was once frowned upon to be in an unmarried relationship or have a child out of wedlock. Thankfully, those days are gone forever as most people are now free to choose who they want to be with.

When is it time to end the relationship?

1.   When your partner is abusive.

2.   When you don't love your partner anymore.

3.   When your partner isn't ready or willing to change their jealous ways.

Abuse

"What I fear most is power with impunity. I fear
abuse of power, and the power to abuse."
Isabel Allende.

What is abuse? Abuse is when someone intentionally hurts you physically or mentally. There are three basic types of abuse; physical, sexual and emotional abuse. For the purpose of this book we will be focusing on physical and emotional abuse in the context of jealousy. Abuse in any form, physical or mental should never be tolerated: **Does your partner shout at you often? Does your partner display controlling behaviour? Does your partner blame you for their jealous behaviour? Has your partner ever physically attacked you?** If your partner's personality or behaviour relates to any of the above, then you are in an abusive relationship and it's time to get out. Emotional abuse can be the hardest to self-diagnose, often it takes someone else outside the relationship, like a friend or a family member to point out that the relationship is in fact abusive and toxic.

Abusive relationships don't happen overnight, they develop slowly and gradually until the negativity spreads and takes over the relationship.

Signs of abuse:

- Do you feel down and depressed when you are around your partner?

- Do you feel uncomfortable or intimidated when you are around your partner?

Learn to trust your inner gut feelings, they are normally based on facts hidden just below your conscious threshold. You shouldn't feel uncomfortable, depressed or intimidated around your partner; these are all signs that something isn't right. Sadly, we hear all too often in the news stories of women and men who have been attacked and sometimes killed because of a jealous partner.

Staying in an abusive relationship is detrimental to your physical and mental health, which over time will begin to deteriorate the longer you stay in it.

When The Love Has Died

There may come a time in your relationship where the love you once felt for your partner has dwindled. The reasons why your feelings have changed aren't as important, what is important however, is accepting those feelings and addressing them in a constructive way.

We must accept the fact that love doesn't always last forever. People change. Our partners change. We change. For instance, you aren't the same person you were ten years ago and in another ten years' time you won't be the same person as you are today. Everybody changes. Just because we loved our partner six months ago, doesn't necessarily mean that we will still love them in another six months' time. Those things that we once liked and loved about our partner, may now be the things that we dislike the most. **When the love has withered and died, it's time to accept it so that we can move forward with our life.**

Signs you have fallen out of love:

- Do you find communication with your partner difficult?

- Do you have less and less things in common between you and your partner as time goes by?

- Do you go out of your way to spend less time with your partner?

- Do you find your partner unattractive?

- Do you fantasise about being with someone else?

If you are experiencing any of the above signs, then it may be time to end the relationship.

Not Ready & Willing

How can you help someone who doesn't want to be helped? The answer is of course, you can't. You can't make anyone change unless they want to change themselves. **If your partner isn't ready or willing to change their jealous ways then sadly, there is nothing that you nor anyone else can do to help them.** Your partner must be ready and willing to change before you can help them become jealousy free.

How can you tell if your partner isn't ready and willing to change their jealous ways? One of the easiest ways of finding out is to simply ask your partner.

Dave says, *"Susan, I'm not happy with the direction our relationship seems to be heading. I love you and I don't want us to separate but, unless you're willing to change your jealous ways, I'm struggling to see a future for us. Do you want to change?"*

If your partner says YES, then you and your partner have something to work with. If your partner says NO, then it's time to face facts and maybe even consider ending the relationship. It may sound like an extreme reaction however, the alternative of stopping with someone who is suffering with jealousy and doesn't want to change their ways will ultimately end in your unhappiness. A happy and secure relationship is fundamentally based on trust, without trust there is nothing but fear and misery.

Signs that your partner isn't ready or willing to change:

- They blame you for their jealousy.

- They are comfortable with the state of the relationship as it is.

- They won't accept that they have a problem.

- They want you to change.

- They aren't willing to change.

It's a sad fact of life that some people don't want to change or are not ready to change because they are content with their life and the way they are. If your partner is one of those people, then you have to consider if you can see a future with them. Staying with a partner who isn't ready or willing to change their ways will do nothing but drag you down, until eventually you hit bottom yourself. **Don't allow that to happen to you, you deserve to be in a jealousy free relationship.**

How To End The Relationship

Choosing to end a relationship can be one of the most difficult and stressful decisions that you will ever have to make. **Let's make no bones about it, it's never easy, it's going to hurt and there is no pain-free way of doing it.** Once you have decided that it's time to end the relationship, it's then time to prepare for the end. Begin by writing a list of all the reasons why you want to end the relationship, this is so that you can be clear in your own mind why you are choosing to end the relationship.

Jane's List:

- I'm not happy.

- He makes me feel frightened.

- I don't love him anymore.

- He doesn't respect me.

- There's no trust in the relationship.

- I'm sick of all the stress and worry.

- I want to be happy.

Once you have written your list you can then begin to identify all the reasons in your mind, why you are making this difficult decision and why it's the correct one for you. The process of writing down these reasons will help your mind come to terms with the possibility of separation. **When you have come to terms with the reasons why it's in your best interest to end the relationship, it will make the endeavour of separating from your partner far easier.**

It's now time to talk to your partner, decide on a date and a suitable place to break the news. If your partner is abusive or manipulative then it may be a good idea to end the relationship in a public place, somewhere where you can feel safe, this way if your partner does become aggressive you can get up and leave. However, if you are concerned for your safety then ending the relationship over the phone may be the safest option. **It's important to remember that if you are at this stage in your relationship, it shouldn't come as a complete surprise to your partner.**

When telling your partner your decision to end the relationship be gentle but resolute in your decision. Don't give them mixed signals, be honest but not unkind. Don't allow yourself to get drawn into an argument about who's right and who's wrong, this will just delay the process and take you back to square one. Accept some responsibility for how the relationship has turned out but remember you are not RESPONSIBLE for your partner's happiness; you are only responsible for your own happiness. Once you have broken the news you need to lay out some boundaries about future contact between you.

If you live together then you must decide between you who is going to move out. If you believe that your partner won't move out, then you must consider where you'll be able to go. **If you have children together it's imperative that you make contingency plans before you break the news to your partner.**

Once you have told your partner your decision to end the relationship, you'll both need time to heal. Every relationship is different, and every person is different. You probably won't be able to be friends right away; this will take time and space.

Talk to your friends and family, don't try to get through this significant time on your own.

When It's Time To End The Relationship

1. If your partner is abusive or you don't love your partner anymore due to their jealous ways, then it's time to end the relationship.

2. Making the decision to end a relationship is one of the hardest decisions you can make.

3. Abuse is when someone intentionally hurts you, physically or mentally.

4. Staying in an abusive relationship is detrimental to your physical and mental health.

5. Learn to trust your inner feelings.

6. You can't help anyone to change unless they want to change themselves.

7. A happy and secure relationship is fundamentally based on trust, without it there is nothing but fear and misery.

8. Ending a relationship is going to hurt but unfortunately there is no pain-free way of doing it.

9. You must be clear in your own mind why you are choosing to end the relationship.

10. Decide on a date and a time to break the news.

When You Change, Your Partner Has To Change

"If you don't like something, change it. If you can't change it, change your attitude."

Maya Angelou.

Essentially, if you want your partner to act differently towards you, you have to treat yourself differently first. By changing yourself first you are setting a precedent and leading the way for the change you so desire in your partner. **Your external world is a reflection of your internal world.**

When you mentally make the decision to change, your partner and therefore your relationship, will also naturally change. Have you ever experienced a situation where you finally decided that enough was enough and things must change and because you made that decision things did change? Maybe it happened when you were at school and the school bully thought it would be fun to torment you but one day the bully pushed you too far and you snapped. You let loose giving the bully a run for their money and in that moment the bully saw a different you because you had changed. After that the bully began to treat you differently because you weren't an easy target anymore. **When you change, the people around you change.** The same principle runs throughout all areas of your life, if you want your partner to change and become jealousy free, then you have to make the changes first. **We are, what we think, not what we think we are.**

Dave says, *"After a few months of being with Susan, I noticed that she was trying to change me. She wanted me to be home by a certain time. She wanted me to call her throughout the day. It was like living by a stopwatch and if ever I was even just thirty minutes late, it was like...* **"Where have you been, why are you so late?"** *...My life suddenly became a living hell. Until one day I changed, I decided that enough was enough and I decided to tell Susan how I felt. I told her that I couldn't cope with her jealous ways and that I was sick and tired of it all. I told her that I was not prepared to be in a relationship where I felt like I was under lock and key. I told her that things had to change. She had to change. After I told Susan how I felt, Susan began to change. She didn't give me such a hard time and our relationship became a lot better."*

In the example above Dave decided that things had to change and because Dave changed, Susan had to change to save their relationship. **When you change, your partner has to change. When you get serious about changing your** relationship, your partner has to get serious about changing their behaviour.

What Example Are You Setting?

"If we lose love and self-respect for each other, this is how we finally die."

Maya Angelou.

YOUR PARTNER CAN ONLY TREAT YOU, THE WAY THAT YOU ALLOW THEM TO TREAT YOU! Your relationship with your partner, work colleagues, neighbours, friends and even your relationship with your own family is based upon the relationship that you have with yourself. **In life people will generally treat you the way you treat yourself and the way that you treat yourself is down to your self-image.**

As a child, Susan was close to her parents, she loved her mother dearly. Susan's mother mollycoddled Susan allowing her free rein to get away with almost anything whenever her father wasn't around. She was allowed to watch whatever she wanted on TV, she stayed out until late at night, she was even allowed to get away with the odd curse word. Susan's relationship with her father on the other hand, was totally different. Her father never allowed her to watch any TV that he deemed inappropriate and whenever he wasn't working late, Susan had to be home before eight and never used curse words in front of her father. What made Susan change her behaviour? She loved to watch scary, violent films. She revelled in staying out until late with her friends and she became highly skilled in the use of profanities. Susan changed her behaviour to accommodate her parents EXPECTATIONS of her. Your partner will not treat you the way you WISH to be treated; your partner will only treat you the way you EXPECT to be treated. **A wish and an expectation are fundamentally different. A wish is nothing more than a great desire that something will happen, an expectation is a confident assumption, that something will happen. When you change, your partner will change.**

As a rule of thumb:

- If you respect yourself, your partner will also respect you.

- If you don't respect yourself, your partner won't respect you.

- If you love yourself, your partner will also love you.

- If you don't love yourself, your partner won't love you.

- If you treat yourself well, your partner will also treat you well.

- If you don't treat yourself well, your partner won't treat you well.

If you're at your wits end because of your partner's jealous ways, then it's time to take some of that responsibility on yourself. **Remember, your partner can only treat you the way that you allow them to treat you.** Your outer world is a reflection of your inner world. When you start treating yourself with respect and love and know unreservedly within yourself that you deserve to be treated with love and respect, your partner will have no choice other than to start treating you with love and respect, if they wish to be part of your life. **Sometimes in life you have to act the way you want to become, until you become the way you act. If you want your partner to treat you differently, then you have to treat yourself differently.**

Have High Expectations

Ask Yourself These Fundamental Questions:

- Do I treat myself well?
- Do I respect myself?
- Do I like myself?

When you begin to treat yourself well, you will automatically expect to be treated well. You have to teach your partner how to treat you, you have to show them what is acceptable behaviour and what isn't. You must become that positive example for your partner to follow. Your self-image whether it be positive or negative, will be reflected in your life through your personality and your behaviour. Other people, especially your partner will pick up on your self-image and how you treat yourself. Your partner's behaviour, be it negative or positive will be greatly influenced by your behaviour towards yourself. **You cannot expect your partner to treat you any differently to the way you treat yourself.**

Fundamentally, your self-image reveals to your partner your expectations in life, it reveals your strengths and weaknesses. **If your partner isn't treating you the way you want to be treated, then you have to be honest with yourself and ask the question, "Am I treating myself the way that I want and expect to be treated?"** When you start thinking differently, you will start feeling differently and this new you becomes an integral part of who you are. If your partner, or anyone else for that matter, doesn't treat you the way you expect to be treated, you can then hold that person in your life, to account.

If you lay down, people will walk over you. If you stand tall, no one can walk over you. Once you start giving yourself the respect that you wish from others, your partner will have to follow. Build a foundation of respect and love for yourself that will make it impossible for anyone, including your partner, to take you for granted. Everything that you want on the outside has to originate from the inside.

When You Change, Your Partner Has To Change

1. If you want your partner to be different with you, then you have to become different with yourself first.

2. When you change, other people change.

3. When you get serious about changing your relationship, your partner has to get serious about changing their behaviour.

4. Your partner can only treat you, the way that you allow them to treat you.

5. Your partner will not treat you the way you wish to be treated; your partner will treat you the way you expect to be treated.

6. You cannot expect your partner to treat you any differently to the way you treat yourself.

Bibliography

SHAKESPEARE, William. The Comedy Of Errors,

Schucman Dr. Helen. (scribe) A Course In Miracles, Foundation for inner peace.

HAUCK, Dr Paul. 1993, Jealousy: Why It Happens & How To Overcome It, Sheldon Press.

2017 Film IT

1982 Film E.T.

1991 Film Drop Dead Fred.

1940 Film The Great Dictator

1979 Film Monty Python's Life of Brian

MATTHEWS Andrew. 1989, Being Happy, Seashell Publishers Pty Ltd.

MALTZ, Dr. Maxwell. 1960, Psycho-Cybernetics, pocket Books, New York.

Swindoll Charles R. 1990, The Grace Awakening

2001 Film Shallow Hal

Bandler Dr. Richard. 2008, Guide To Trance Formation, Hci.

Printed by Amazon Italia Logistica S.r.l.
Torrazza Piemonte (TO), Italy

11418021R00119